A SAINSBURY COOKBOOK

A TRAVELLER'S
TASTES

JOSCELINE DIMBLEBY

CONTENTS

Published exclusively for J Sainsbury plc
Stamford House Stamford Street
London SE1 9LL
by Woodhead–Faulkner (Publishers) Ltd
Fitzwilliam House 32 Trumpington Street
Cambridge CB2 1QY

First published 1986

Printed in Great Britain

THE AUTHOR

Josceline Dimbleby's childhood was spent abroad from the age of five, mostly in the Middle East and South America, so that at an early age she learned to appreciate a wide range of food, an interest which has led to this exciting new Sainsbury Cookbook. *A Traveller's Tastes* is an exclusive collection of recipes inspired by her travels in far-flung countries around the world.

Josceline's instinct has always been to create her own recipes, which results in varied and interesting dishes, but leading a very busy life herself she appreciates the value of advance preparation and simple methods.

Josceline has written many cookery articles for the national press and has featured on television and radio. Her first cookery book, *A Taste of Dreams*, appeared in 1976, followed by *Puddings, Desserts and Savouries*, which won the André Simon Award for the best cookery book of 1979. She is currently the cookery correspondent of the *Sunday Telegraph*.

Josceline lives in London with her husband, journalist and broadcaster David Dimbleby, and their three children.

INTRODUCTION

More than any of my others, this book is part of my life. In my English kitchen I have re-created tastes and smells which pinpoint for me some moment in a far-off place. I was brought up travelling and I still travel as much as I possibly can. Living abroad as a child initiated my interest in food, and, if I stopped my regular journeys now, I feel that I would soon become a far less inspired cook.

The food in this book is not traditional and there are no truly authentic dishes, although many of the flavours will, I hope, be vividly evocative to fellow travellers. For me the bonus of experiencing different cuisines is that they can suggest new methods of cooking and combining ingredients so that, using my imagination in conjunction with my memories, I can make a dish which I feel is absolutely personal. This is surely the basis on which the best of the world's cuisines have evolved: they are all the result of cultural mixtures and foreign influences. So, returning from my travels, the prospect of being back in my kitchen and casting a new eye on familiar ingredients which I have bought round the corner always excites me.

I have loved working on this book. It has made me read through my diaries and notes and so remember not only food but places, people and events which I haven't thought about for years. For some of the recipes, on the other hand the ideas are very recent; several came from a journey in India early this year.

Meals become particularly important when they punctuate a journey and food is a marvellous interest for the traveller. Wherever you go you will find people eager to discuss their food; it is a subject which unites strangers and helps form the fastest friendships. The best thing to me is that there are so many places still to be explored, and that from the most unlikely spot there will always be the gist of an idea which may one day take shape in my kitchen.

Note on recipes
All recipes in this book give ingredients in both metric (g, ml, etc.) and imperial (oz, pints, etc.) measures. Use either set of quantities, but not both, in any one recipe. All teaspoons and tablespoons are level unless otherwise stated. Egg size is medium (size 3) unless otherwise stated. Preparation and cooking times are given as a guideline: all timings are approximate.

FRANCE

VEAL BLANQUETTE PAPRIKA

Preparation time: 30 minutes + 1½ hours cooking   Serves 4

1 large red pepper

3–4 cloves of garlic

25 g (1 oz) butter

1 tablespoon olive oil

500 g (1 lb) stewing veal or
boneless pork steaks, cubed

2 teaspoons paprika

2 good pinches of cayenne
pepper

25 g (1 oz) plain flour

450 ml (¾ pint) milk

2 tablespoons lemon juice

2 teaspoons green
peppercorns

125 g (4 oz) button
mushrooms

125 g (4 oz) frozen petits
pois

150 ml (5 fl oz) carton of
soured cream or natural
yogurt

Oven temperature:
Gas Mark 2/150°C/300°F

I always think of 'blanquette de veau' as an old-fashioned dish; perhaps because it was one of the first things I learned to make. In any case it is a simply-made and comforting casserole. My version here is a cross between a blanquette and a veal goulash, so it is influenced by both France and Hungary. The red pepper and garlic melt in the sauce as it cooks and the result is smooth and mild. Serve it with plenty of rice, either white long-grained or brown.

Preheat the oven. Cut the pepper in half, remove the seeds and slice it as thinly as possible. Peel the garlic and cut the cloves in half. Melt the butter and olive oil over a medium heat in an iron or other flameproof casserole dish on top of the stove. Add the veal and stir it around just to seal the outside lightly. Then add the paprika, the cayenne pepper and the garlic. Stir and remove from the heat. Stir the flour into the meat and then gradually add the milk, followed by the lemon juice. Add the green peppercorns and the sliced pepper. Return to the heat and bring to the boil, stirring. Bubble, still stirring, for 2 minutes. Then cover the dish and cook it in the centre of the oven for about 1½ hours or until the meat is tender.

Remove the casserole from the oven and add the mushrooms and petits pois. Bring back to bubbling on top of the stove, cover again and simmer very gently for 5 minutes. Just before serving, spoon the soured cream or yogurt on to the casserole but don't stir it in.

LEEK AND PARSNIP SOUP

Preparation time: 15 minutes + 20 minutes cooking   Serves 4

75 g (3 oz) butter

250 g (8 oz) parsnips,
peeled and chopped

500 g (1 lb) leeks, trimmed
and sliced roughly

600 ml (1 pint) chicken stock

450 ml (¾ pint) milk

1 tablespoon lemon juice

150 ml (5 fl oz) carton of
single cream

2 good tablespoons chopped
chives

salt and black pepper

There is no need to wonder where the inspiration for this soup came from: it is, of course, a version of one of France's most famous soups, Vichyssoise. I have had many different versions of it in France, ranging from a thick, steaming-hot, homely mixture to something chilled and delicate with a satin-smooth texture. This recipe, in which I use parsnips instead of potatoes for their lovely sweet taste, veers towards the homely, being a good family soup to have for lunch with crusty bread.

Heat the butter in a large, heavy-based saucepan over a medium heat. Add the chopped vegetables and stir them around in the butter for about 5 minutes. Then add the chicken stock, cover the saucepan and simmer the contents gently for 15–20 minutes, until the vegetables are tender.

Pour the soup into a food processor or liquidiser and whizz it until smooth. Pour the purée back into the saucepan and stir in the milk. Season to taste with salt and black pepper. Reheat the soup gently and then stir in the lemon juice. Just before serving roughly mix in the cream and the chopped chives.

STUFFED SARDINES

Preparation time: 30 minutes + 15 minutes baking   Serves 4–5

1 tablespoon olive oil, plus a
little extra

2 cloves of garlic, chopped
finely

350 g (12 oz) chicory, sliced
thinly

about 8 large lettuce leaves,
chopped small

grated rind of 1 small orange

A great friend of mine has a pretty pink-washed farmhouse in Provence. A long straight avenue of chestnut trees leads up to it. Once, arriving for lunch on a baking-hot day, we stopped the car at the bottom of the avenue and decided to walk up to the house under the shade of the trees. Immediately we got out of the car we knew what we were having for lunch: fresh sardines. The smell of sardines grilling, the most common method of cooking them, is powerful; appetising yet pervasive. The taste is delicious. Now that it is easier to buy large fresh sardines in this

2 teaspoons caster sugar

8 fresh sardines, about 20–25 cm (8–10 inches) long

25 g (1 oz) fresh breadcrumbs

25 g (1 oz) grated cheese

salt and black pepper

Oven temperature:
Gas Mark 9/240°C/475°F

country there is another way to cook them: stuffing them and baking in the oven, which minimises the smell and makes a refreshing change.

Preheat the oven. Heat the olive oil in a largish frying pan over a medium heat. Add the chopped garlic, stir for a moment and then add the sliced chicory. Stir around with a wooden spoon for 4–5 minutes until the vegetables are softened. Stir in the chopped lettuce and then add the orange rind and the caster sugar and fry for a moment more. Remove the pan from the heat, season to taste with salt and black pepper and leave it to cool.

Meanwhile, wash the sardines, rubbing off any scales with your fingers. Carefully cut open the abdomen from below the head to the tail. If they are not already cleaned, remove the innards with your fingers under running water and pinch off the heads. Pull back the flesh of the fish away from the bones (diagram 1) and gently pull out the backbone (diagram 2), breaking it off above the tail. Take each fillet and spoon some of the cool filling on to the flesh side (diagram 3). Fold the fish lightly together – the filling will be bursting out as in diagram 4 – and very carefully put them in a large gratin dish. If there is any filling left over, spoon it evenly into the fish to fill them even more. Mix the breadcrumbs and cheese together in a bowl and scatter them over the fish. Dribble a little olive oil over the top. Put the dish towards the top of the oven and bake for 15 minutes.

1

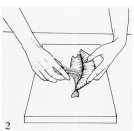
2

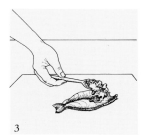
3

4

YELLOW PEPPER TART

Preparation time: 30 minutes + 25 minutes baking   Serves 6

150 ml (¼ pint) milk

2 pinches of saffron threads
or 1 packet of powdered
saffron

125 g (4 oz) semolina

125 g (4 oz) plain flour

125 g (4 oz) butter

1 tablespoon water

2 tablespoons olive oil

750 g (1½ lb) yellow
peppers, de-seeded and
chopped fairly small

1 red pepper, de-seeded and
chopped fairly small

2 cloves of garlic, peeled and
chopped finely

2 egg yolks

*This shallow tart is inspired by the Pissaladière of
Provence but it has quite a different filling: sweet
yellow peppers bound with an egg and saffron cream.
You can, of course, make the tart with peppers of any
colour, but there are moments of the year when the
shops seem to be full of beautiful yellow ones, which I
always think taste particularly mild and sweet. I
usually include one red pepper as well, because it looks
so pretty speckled in the rich yellow. The semolina
gives the pastry a crisp and light texture. I often serve
the tart with a green salad for a light lunch but it also
makes a good hot first course, in which case it would
serve up to eight people. You can also serve it cold.*

Preheat the oven. Bring the milk to the boil and
pour it on to the saffron in a bowl. Stir, and leave
on one side. Put the semolina and flour into a
bowl and mix them. Gently melt the butter,
with the water, in a saucepan; then pour the
liquid on to the flour, mixing it in with a wooden
spoon. Take bits of the dough and press them
evenly round the sides and over the bottom of a

Stuffed Sardines

| 1 large egg (size 1–2) |
| 2 teaspoons caster sugar |
| salt and black pepper |

Oven temperature:
Gas Mark 7/220°C/425°F

25 cm (10-inch) loose-based fluted aluminium flan tin, and then refrigerate the flan case.

Heat the olive oil over a medium heat and add the chopped peppers and garlic. Cook, stirring frequently, for 10–15 minutes or until the peppers are soft and then leave on one side to cool slightly. Whisk the egg yolks and the egg together in a mixing bowl, and then whisk in the saffron milk and season with salt and black pepper. Stir in the cooled pepper and garlic and then pour the mixture into the chilled pastry case. Level the surface and sprinkle it with the caster sugar. Cook the tart towards the top of the oven for about 25 minutes until it is just set in the middle and speckles of black have appeared on the peppers.

Push the tart carefully up out of the tin and on to a serving plate. As the pastry is very crumbly, however, you will probably want to keep it on the tin base. You can keep the tart warm in a low oven or re-heat it later.

Onion Tart with Olive Pastry

Yellow Pepper Tart

9

ONION TART WITH OLIVE PASTRY

Preparation time: 1 hour + 30 minutes baking   Serves 6

For the pastry:

175 g (6 oz) plain flour

1 teaspoon salt

5 tablespoons extra virgin olive oil

1 tablespoon water

2 cloves of garlic, crushed

For the filling:

3 tablespoons extra-virgin olive oil

750 g (1½ lb) French or Spanish red onions, sliced very thinly

25 g (1 oz) black olives, stoned and chopped finely

250 ml (8 fl oz) double cream

1 egg

2 egg yolks

salt and black pepper

Oven temperatures:
Gas Mark 7/220°C/425°F
Gas Mark 5/190°C/375°F

All over France you will find different versions of Tarte à l'Oignon and almost all are delicious. I much prefer a pure onion tart to any other combination. For my personal version I use pastry made with olive oil, which is something I tried when I had brought back some oil from Provence. It is particularly good for tart crusts because it can be baked blind, keeps its shape well and retains its crispness, while adding a subtle, southern flavour of olives to the pastry. With a green salad this makes an excellent light lunch.

Preheat the oven to the higher setting. To make the pastry, sift the flour and salt into a bowl. Put the olive oil and water into a saucepan and add the crushed garlic. Heat for a minute or two until just beginning to bubble. Add the hot liquid gradually to the flour, stirring it in with a wooden spoon. Using your fingers, press pieces of the crumbly dough firmly against the sides of a 24 cm (9½-inch) fluted, loose-based aluminium flan tin. Then press the remaining dough evenly over the base of the tin. Refrigerate the pastry case while you make the filling.

Heat the olive oil in a large frying pan over a gentle heat. Add the sliced onions and cook slowly, stirring around often, until completely soft but not browned at all. Stir in the chopped olives and remove from the heat.

Cook the unfilled pastry case in the centre of the oven for 10–15 minutes. Then remove from the oven and turn down the heat to the lower setting. In a mixing bowl, finish the filling. Whisk the cream well with the egg and egg yolks and season with salt and black pepper. Stir the cooked onions into the cream and pour the mixture into the pastry case. Put it back in the centre of the oven for 25–35 minutes until the centre of the filling is only just set.

RABBIT AND PUMPKIN WITH MUSTARD AND WHITE KIDNEY BEANS

Preparation time: 20 minutes + 1¾ hours cooking   Serves 4

1 tablespoon olive oil

2 teaspoons caraway seeds

750–875 g (1½–1¾ lb) fresh rabbit joints

4 cloves of garlic, chopped roughly

125 g (4 oz) butter

1 kg (2 lb) piece of pumpkin, peeled, de-seeded and chopped

2 teaspoons green peppercorns, crushed

4 teaspoons Dijon mustard

a little more than 150 ml (¼ pint) white wine or water

400 g (14 oz) can of white kidney beans (cannellini beans)

150 ml (5 fl oz) carton of soured cream

continental parsley

salt

Oven temperature:
Gas Mark 4/180°C/350°F

Rabbit seems to be eaten much more in France than in England, where people often look rather apprehensive if you suggest having rabbit for supper. But since it is possible to buy excellent fresh rabbit nowadays, I think one should disregard any hesitation and show people how good it can be. In France, more often than not, it is cooked with mustard, which certainly goes well with rabbit and for this casserole I have added a base of pumpkin purée flavoured with caraway seeds.

Preheat the oven. Heat the olive oil in a largish iron or other flameproof casserole over a medium heat, add the caraway seeds and stir them around for a moment. Then add the rabbit joints and seal them on both sides. Stir in the chopped garlic, stir around for half a minute and then turn off the heat. Add the butter, cut into pieces. When the butter has melted in the hot casserole, add the chopped pumpkin, the crushed green peppercorns, the mustard, the white wine or water and a sprinkling of salt. Stir with a wooden spoon to mix thoroughly. Cover the casserole with a tight-fitting lid and cook it in the centre of the oven for 1¼ hours.

Stir the casserole with a wooden spoon to break up the pumpkin until it becomes a purée. Drain the canned kidney beans and add them to the dish. Cover the dish again and continue cooking in the oven for another 20–30 minutes. Just before serving, pour the soured cream roughly over the top and sprinkle with a few whole leaves of continental parsley, if available, or ordinary parsley.

CHICKEN BAKED IN A SALT CRUST WITH ROSE-TINTED SAUCE

Preparation time: 5 minutes + 2 hours baking + 15 minutes   Serves 4–5

1.25–1.5 kg (2½–3 lb) fresh chicken (corn fed if possible)

6 cloves of garlic, peeled and chopped roughly

coarse salt

For the sauce:

750 g (1½ lb) tomatoes

50 g (2 oz) butter

2.5 cm (1-inch) piece of fresh ginger, peeled and chopped finely

150 ml (5 fl oz) carton of double cream

salt

cayenne pepper

Oven temperature:
Gas Mark 8/230°C/450°F

The simple method of baking in salt is thought to originate, as do so many clever ways of cooking, in China. These days, however, the place you would be most likely to find a perfect chicken or fish prepared in this way would be in France, or possibly Spain. Don't imagine that the chicken turns out at all salty to taste; the salt simply acts as an insulating crust and cooks the bird to a perfection hard to achieve in any other way. You need quite a lot of coarse salt to bury the bird with, but you can keep the salt to use again; once you have used this method I feel sure you will want to repeat it. In fact I use the very coarse salt which I buy in huge bags for my dishwasher.

Preheat the oven. Choose a deep, ovenproof casserole in which the chicken will fit with 2.5–5 cm (1–2 inches) to spare all around it. Line the base of the dish with two layers of foil, bringing it up well over the edges. Put the chopped garlic into the body cavity of the chicken. Put a thickish layer of coarse salt into the dish, put the chicken in breast-side downwards and then pour in enough salt to bury the bird completely. Cover the dish tightly and then put it in the centre of the oven for about 2 hours or until cooked.

Shortly before the chicken is cooked, make the sauce. Put the tomatoes into a bowl, pour boiling water over them, leave for a minute, and then drain and peel the tomatoes and chop them up very small. Melt the butter in a heavy saucepan over a medium heat. Add the chopped ginger and the tomatoes and bubble them gently in the open saucepan, stirring frequently, for 10–15 minutes until they are cooked and mushy. Put the pan on one side.

When the chicken is ready take the dish out of the oven and spoon the top layer of salt into a

Chicken Baked in a Salt Crust with Rose-tinted Sauce
Rabbit and Pumpkin with Mustard and White Kidney Beans

large bowl; then lift out the chicken with the help of the foil, tipping all the rest of the salt into the bowl as you do so. Wipe any grains of salt off the chicken and put it on a serving dish in a low oven to keep warm while you finish the sauce. Using a wooden spoon rub the tomato and ginger thoroughly through a sieve into another saucepan. Stir in the cream and boil, stirring, for 3–4 minutes until the sauce is slightly thickened. Remove it from the heat and season to taste with salt and cayenne pepper. Just before serving pour the sauce evenly all over the chicken.

TARTE À L'ORANGE

Preparation time: 30 minutes + 1 hour chilling + 45 minutes baking   Serves 6

For the pastry:

250 g (8 oz) plain flour, plus extra for rolling

50 g (2 oz) caster sugar

½ teaspoon salt

125 g (4 oz) unsalted butter, plus extra for greasing

1 large egg (size 1–2), whisked

For the filling:

5 oranges

a little milk

2 egg yolks

1 large egg (size 1–2)

75 g (3 oz) + 1 tablespoon caster sugar

salt

Oven temperatures:
Gas Mark 8/230°C/450°F
Gas Mark 4/180°C/350°F

Few things could be more pleasant during the summer than sitting on a terrace in Provence in the dappled shade of an old fig tree, ending a perfect lunch with a slice of Tarte à L'Orange. This peaceful memory is what prompted me to repeat the tarte as I remembered it. Tarte au Citron had long been a favourite and I had never imagined that a tart made from oranges could be quite so good. But both tarts, with their crisp biscuit-like pastry case, light and creamy centre and tangy slices of fruit on top, seemed to me to be equally good.

To make the pastry, sift the flour, the caster sugar and the salt into a bowl. Cut the butter into small pieces and rub it into the flour with your fingertips until the mixture is the texture of breadcrumbs. Then stir in the whisked egg with a fork. Press the mixture with your hands until it sticks together in a piece; then cut it into four and press it together again with your hands. Repeat this three more times, and then press the dough into a ball, cover it with cling film and leave it to rest in the fridge for an hour or more. Then preheat the oven to the first setting.

Butter a 24–25 cm (9½–10-inch) loose-based, fluted, aluminium flan tin. Take the pastry from the fridge and knead it briefly before rolling it out on a floured surface into a piece big

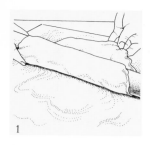

1

2

3

enough to line the flan tin; if the pastry breaks up, just press it together again. Roll the piece of pastry back over the rolling pin (diagram 1) and lift it on to the flan tin (diagram 2). Fold the edges back in to make a double thickness of pastry round the sides (diagram 3), pushing it a little above the top of the flan tin, and evening up the edges with pieces of pastry if necessary. Prick the base lightly all over with a fork. Lay a sheet of foil over the pastry and put a layer of dried beans or rice all over the base. Make sure that the foil comes up over the edges of the pastry to stop them getting too brown during the cooking. Bake the pastry case blind in the centre of the oven for 25 minutes, turning the flan round once during the cooking.

Meanwhile, prepare the filling. Finely grate the zest of 1 orange and put it into a pouring saucepan. Put the juice of 2 oranges into a measuring jug and make it up to 150 ml (¼ pint) with milk. Pour this on to the grated zest. In a mixing bowl, lightly whisk the egg yolks and the whole egg with the 75 g (3 oz) caster sugar and a little salt. Bring the orange juice and milk to the boil, let it bubble for a minute and then pour the boiling liquid on to the eggs in a steady stream, whisking all the time.

When the pastry case is ready, turn the oven down to the second setting and pour the egg and orange mixture into the cooked pastry case. Put it back in the oven for 15–20 minutes, until just set. With a sharp knife slice the remaining 3 unpeeled oranges across in the thinnest possible slices, removing any pips. Blanch the slices in a saucepan of boiling water for 1 minute, and then drain and pat them dry with kitchen paper. Arrange the orange slices on top of the tart, bringing them right over the edges of the pastry. Heat the grill to its highest heat. Sprinkle the tablespoon of caster sugar evenly over the oranges and put the tart briefly under the grill quite near the heat, until the oranges have browned in patches. Push the tart out of the flan tin and slide it carefully off the base on to a serving plate. Eat it hot or cold, but not chilled.

15

PROVENÇAL PRUNE TART

Preparation time: 10 minutes + 30 minutes resting
+ 20 minutes baking

Serves 6

250 g (8 oz) packet of puff
pastry, fresh or frozen and
thawed

flour for rolling

15 g (½ oz) soft butter or
margarine, plus extra for
greasing

2½ tablespoons caster sugar

125 g (4 oz) soft pitted
prunes

Oven temperature:
Gas Mark 7/220°C/425°F

One summer, we spent a perfect holiday in a
farmhouse set amongst the theatrical-looking rocky
Alpilles in Provence. It was my annual break from
cooking, so we tried out all the surrounding family
restaurants. On our last night, however, we treated
ourselves to a less modest establishment and finished
the meal with a wonderful Tarte aux Pruneaux
which was simply a few prunes scattered between thin,
crisp layers of the flakiest pastry. I tried to imitate it
when we got home and found that I achieved a rather
amazing result very easily by using ready-made puff
pastry.

Cut the pastry in half and form the halves into
balls. Roll them out thinly on a floured surface
into two roughly circular shapes about 25–28 cm
(10–11 inches) in diameter. Smear one circle all
over with the butter or margarine and sprinkle it
evenly with 2 tablespoons of caster sugar,
through a sieve. Cut the soft prunes in half
crossways and flatten them slightly with your
fingers. Arrange them on the butter and sugar,
spaced apart and leaving about 2 cm (¾ inch)
around the edge. Lay the second circle of pastry
on top and roll over the edges all round to seal
them. Place carefully on a large, buttered, flat tin
plate or baking sheet. Rest the tart in the fridge
for 30 minutes or more, and, meanwhile,
preheat the oven.

Brush the top of the tart lightly with cold
water and sprinkle the remaining caster sugar
evenly all over it through a sieve. Bake the tart
towards the top of the oven for 15–20 minutes
until it is really blackened on top.

Note: a good substitute for the French *crème
fraîche* to serve with this tart is 150 ml (5 fl oz)
carton of double cream, whipped until it is thick
but not stiff, with 4 tablespoons of natural
yogurt then folded into it. An alternative would
be Sainsbury's natural fromage frais.

Tarte à l'Orange ➤
Provençal Prune Tart

SPAIN

CHILLED ALMOND AND GARLIC SOUP

Preparation time: 10 minutes + 35 minutes cooking + chilling   Serves 4

1 large head of garlic

1 large spanish onion, chopped roughly

900 ml (1½ pints) milk

125 g (4 oz) ground almonds

the juice of 1 small lemon

2 teaspoons paprika

3–4 pinches of cayenne pepper

salt

When you spend some time in Spain you soon discover that a garlic soup doesn't taste strongly of garlic. Garlic is only really pervasive when it is raw or only briefly cooked; longer cooking brings out its sweet, mild flavour and smooth consistency. There are all sorts of garlic soups in Spain, some with almonds in them, some not, but in my experience they are always served hot. My version, which is a beautiful creamy white, is chilled instead and I find it extremely popular. A bright red whirl of paprika, lemon juice and cayenne is dribbled on top of the white soup.

Separate the garlic cloves from the head and peel them. Put the garlic cloves and the chopped onion into a largish saucepan and add 300 ml (½ pint) of the milk. Bring to the boil, cover the pan and then simmer very gently for 20–25 minutes until the onions and garlic are very soft. Pour into a food processor, add the ground almonds and whizz until you have a smooth paste. Turn the paste back into the saucepan and stir in the remaining 600 ml (1 pint) milk. Season generously with salt. Bring to the boil, stirring all the time, and simmer, still stirring, for 8–10 minutes. Pour into a bowl and leave to cool; then chill in the fridge.

This is meant to be a thick soup, but if it is necessary, you can thin it with a little milk. Then to serve it, mix the lemon juice with the paprika and cayenne pepper in a cup with a teaspoon. Spoon the chilled soup into individual bowls and spoon the lemon and paprika in a whirl on top of the soup in each bowl.

SQUID LEQUEITIO

Preparation time: 50 minutes   Serves 4

2 tablespoons olive oil

500 g (1 lb) spanish onions, very finely chopped

juice of 1 large orange

2 tablespoons tomato purée

150 ml (¼ pint) water

1 kg (2 lb) squid, prepared and cleaned

2 teaspoons dried oregano

salt and cayenne pepper

One hot August I spent a teenage summer holiday with my parents in a village called Lequeitio on the coast of Northern Spain and had my first holiday romance. His name was Dietrich. He was dark and handsome with navy blue eyes. Every evening we danced in the village square and every day we swam together, holding hands. One night he took me to a restaurant where I tasted my first squid, not fried as it usually is in Spain, nor in its rich black ink, but in a sweet onion sauce, flavoured with oregano. This is a recreation of that simple dish. Many people think of squid as having a leathery texture and this is nearly always because of overcooking; sliced squid should have only a few minutes cooking, and it will then be tender and delicious. I like to eat this healthy stew with baked potatoes and a crisp green vegetable.

Heat the olive oil in an iron or other flameproof casserole dish on top of the stove over a medium heat. Add the chopped onions and stir them around for 2 or 3 minutes; then stir in the orange juice, the tomato purée and the water. Cover the pan and cook the sauce over a very low heat for 30–45 minutes until it is soft and mushy.

Meanwhile, make sure the fishmonger has extracted the transparent bone from the squid and taken out all the soft innards. Then slice the bodies of the squid across in thin rings and cut the tentacles up roughly. When the onion sauce is ready, add the squid and the oregano, increase the heat again, cover and cook for another 5 minutes or so until the squid is just opaque. Remove from the heat, season to taste with salt and a pinch or two of cayenne pepper and serve.

ANCHOVY-STUFFED MULLET WITH VEGETABLE STEW

Preparation time: 40 minutes + 20 minutes cooking   Serves 6

2 fairly large aubergines

lemon juice

6 small to medium-size red mullet

50 g (1¾ oz) can of anchovies in oil

3 tablespoons olive oil

2 large cloves of garlic, chopped roughly

350 g (12 oz) tomatoes, chopped fairly small

1 teaspoon caraway seeds

1 teaspoon paprika

500 g (1 lb) french beans, topped and tailed

432 g (15¼ oz) can of chick-peas, drained

300 g (10 oz) large flat mushrooms, sliced thinly

salt and black pepper

The Spaniards so love fish that even the most remote mountain village, far inland, will receive a regular delivery of absolutely fresh fish. One of my greatest pleasures when we lived in Spain one summer was choosing from the huge variety of fish in the market and having long conversations with the stallholders about how best it should be cooked. Red mullet is an excellent and pretty fish, much eaten in Spain. In this recipe, the fish are stuffed with little strips of anchovy and served with a Spanish-style mixture of vegetables: an easy and satisfying dish. I serve it either with baked potatoes or with good, crusty bread, warmed in the oven.

Cut the unpeeled aubergines across into fairly thin slices. Sprinkle them with lemon juice, rub them all over with salt and leave them in a colander in the sink for half an hour.

If the fish have not been prepared by the fishmonger, gut them, but leave the heads on. Wash them well and rub off any scales. Pat them dry with kitchen paper towelling. Using a small sharp knife, cut slanting slits across the fish on both sides about 2 cm (¾-inch) apart. Slice the anchovy fillets into thin strips and slip a slice down each slit in the red mullet. Then smear the fish generously with olive oil and any oil left from the anchovy can.

Rinse the aubergine slices with cold running water to remove all the salt. Put the remaining oil into a large saucepan and heat it over a medium heat; add the garlic and stir it around, then add the tomatoes, the aubergines, the caraway seeds, the paprika and the prepared french beans. Stir around for a minute, cover the saucepan and let it bubble very gently for about 20 minutes until the aubergines are soft and the beans are cooked. Add the drained chick-peas

Anchovy-stuffed Mullet with Vegetable Stew

and the mushrooms to the saucepan and season with salt and black pepper. Cover the saucepan and cook for another five minutes only; remove from the heat.

Heat the grill to high and grill the stuffed fish for 4–5 minutes on each side: they should be speckled brown. To serve, spoon the vegetable stew into a large, shallow, warmed serving dish and then arrange the fish on top.

SPAIN'S FAVOURITE PUDDING

Preparation time: 15 minutes + 1¼ hours baking + chilling   Serves 4

125 g (4 oz) granulated sugar

150 ml (¼ pint) fresh orange juice

finely grated rind and juice of 1 lemon

3 large eggs (size 1–2)

2 egg yolks

50 g (2 oz) caster sugar

600 ml (1 pint) milk

Oven temperature:
Gas Mark 3/170°C/325°F

When you travel in Spain you see the word 'flan' on every restaurant menu. Aged eighteen, I left England to join my sister and a group of friends in Morocco for a summer holiday. I travelled across Spain with my boyfriend in his dilapidated Mini van, but since I knew my mother would worry I told her that we were travelling with some older, married friends of his, and we sent postcards en route signed by all four of us. I remember that I had budgeted £1 a day for the expenses of the journey and luckily this could nearly always include a 'flan' for pudding as it cost only 5 pesetas. 'Flan' means simply crème caramel or caramel custard, and for some odd reason it seems to be an unofficial national pudding in Spain. Made well from fresh eggs and creamy milk it can be exquisite, and I make it in this recipe with a fresh orange-flavoured caramel, and lemon-tinged custard. If you are planning to make a batch of meringues later, add a third egg yolk to the pudding for luxurious creaminess. I have never known a pudding slip down quite so swiftly.

Preheat the oven, placing a deep roasting pan of hot water in the centre. Put the granulated sugar into a saucepan and strain in the orange and lemon juices. Dissolve the sugar in the juices, stirring it over a low heat. Then increase the heat, bring the syrup to the boil and boil it fiercely, still stirring now and then, until the syrup has thickened and turned a rich golden colour; this usually takes about 5 minutes. Remove the pan from the heat at the first hint of

brown and pour the syrup into a 1.2-litre
(2-pint) ovenproof soufflé dish, or into
individual moulds.

Put the eggs and egg yolks in a bowl with the
caster sugar and whisk them together
thoroughly; then whisk in the reserved lemon
rind. Warm the milk in a saucepan and whisk the
warm milk *lightly* into the eggs. Then pour the
milk mixture gently on to the caramel and put
the dish or moulds into the roasting pan of
water. Cook for 1–1¼ hours, when the custard
should be just set and firm to touch in the centre.
It shouldn't be solid but should wobble a little.

Remove the dish or moulds from the oven and
let them cool; then cover them with cling film
and refrigerate until you are ready to eat them.
Just before eating, turn the pudding out on to a
serving dish or dishes, loosening the edges with
a knife if necessary.

CANARY CAKE

Preparation time: 25 minutes + 50 minutes baking　　　　Serves 6–8

For the cake:

butter for greasing

4 large eggs (size 1–2), separated

75 g (3 oz) caster sugar

finely grated rind of 2 large oranges

125 g (4 oz) ground almonds

2 tablespoons hot water

a pinch of salt

For the syrup and banana topping:

juice of 2 large oranges

juice of ½ lemon

75 g (3 oz) demerara sugar

1 teaspoon ground cinnamon

2–3 firm bananas

Oven temperature:
Gas Mark 4/180°C/350°F

About 25 years ago, my parents bought a fisherman's cottage on the remote southern coast of an unknown Canary island. There was no hotel and we were the only foreigners there. I often think of Maria, who cooked for us. One year she made a particularly good pudding-cake for my birthday using local ingredients – almonds, oranges and bananas. This recipe is drawn from my memory of that cake. A good accompaniment to this, if you are using it as a pudding, is a bowl of good vanilla ice cream.

Preheat the oven. Butter a 20 cm (8-inch) cake tin and line it with a disc of buttered greaseproof paper. Put the yolks of the eggs into a mixing bowl with the caster sugar and the grated orange rinds and whisk until they are pale and fluffy. Then whisk in the ground almonds a little at a time, followed by the hot water to soften the mixture. In another bowl, whisk the egg whites with the salt until they stand in soft peaks and then fold them gently into the yolk mixture with a metal spoon. Spoon into the prepared tin and bake the cake in the centre of the oven for 45–50 minutes until it is browned and is resistant to a very light touch in the centre.

Meanwhile, make the syrup. Strain the orange and lemon juice through a sieve into a saucepan and add the demerara sugar and cinnamon. Dissolve the sugar in the juices, stirring it over a low heat. Then increase the heat, boil the syrup briskly for 5 minutes, remove it from the heat, and leave it on one side to cool.

When the cake is ready, leave it in the tin for 10 minutes or so; don't worry if it sinks slightly. Loosen the sides carefully with a knife and turn it out on to a serving plate. Peel the bananas, slice them thinly and arrange the slices over the top of the cake. Immediately spoon the cooled syrup all over the bananas. Keep the cake at room temperature until you want to serve it.

Canary Cake ➤
Spain's Favourite Pudding

24

ITALY

FRANCO'S SPAGHETTI

Preparation time: 15 minutes   Serves 4–5

500 g (1 lb) sprouting broccoli

300 g (10 oz) spaghetti

7 tablespoons virgin olive oil

2–3 cloves of garlic, chopped finely

sea salt and black pepper

To serve:

freshly grated parmesan cheese (optional)

Every April, an Italian friend of ours has a birthday party in his family home which is now run by his brother as a hotel. One year we took the children, and drove all the way from London to Positano for the event. It was well worth the long drive, for Franco celebrates his birthday with a Sagra della Pasta or pasta feast. And feast it was: 40 different kinds of pasta dishes, to be exact. Some of the dishes were elaborate, some simple. Franco's favourite was an unpretentious but delicious spaghetti with sprouting broccoli which he cooks himself at home.

Wash the broccoli and cut it into 1 cm (½-inch) pieces, discarding any hard, thick stalks. Put a little salted water in a saucepan and bring it to the boil. Add the broccoli, cover the pan and boil for only 2 minutes. Drain. Put a large pan of salted water on to the boil and when boiling, add the spaghetti. Meanwhile, heat the olive oil in a large frying pan, add the garlic and cook over a low heat for a minute or two until just browned. Add the broccoli and stir it around over the heat for a minute. Sprinkle with sea salt and plenty of black pepper and turn off the heat.

The spaghetti should be ready in 7–10 minutes, perhaps less if it is fresh; it should be cooked through but still with a slight bite to it. Drain it, rinse it through with running hot water and put it into a warmed serving bowl. Mix in the broccoli and garlic and serve immediately. Have sea salt and black pepper grinders on the table to season if needed, and a bowl of freshly grated parmesan cheese to sprinkle over if you like.

CALVES' LIVER PAR EXCELLENCE

Preparation time: 10 minutes + 10 minutes cooking   Serves 3–4

---

500 g (1 lb) calves' liver

125 g (4 oz) plain flour

1 teaspoon paprika

25 g (1 oz) butter

1 tablespoon olive oil

150 ml (¼ pint) unsweetened apple juice

150 ml (5 fl oz) carton of double cream

a handful of parsley, chopped

salt and black pepper

Both lamb's and calves' liver need only a moment's cooking. The other important thing – which I believe, though butchers tell me it should make no difference – is the colour of the liver: in my experience the paler the liver the more mild and tender it is.

The best calves' liver I have ever eaten was not, as you might imagine, in Italy, but in Switzerland. My parents were living in Berne and when I came out for the school holidays the first thing I would ask for was the wonderful calves' liver, either simply grilled or, even better, accompanied by a slightly sweet, creamy sauce. In this recipe the sauce is made with apple juice and cream. The whole dish takes only minutes to produce and is a perfect meal after a long, busy day. Serve it with either baked or mashed potatoes and a crisp green vegetable.

Peel off any of the thin, transparent skin which may be on the sides of the liver and, if it is not already thinly sliced, slice it as thinly as you can, using a very sharp knife. Cut out any gristly tubes. Put the flour, the paprika and a sprinkling of salt and black pepper into a plastic bag and shake them up together. Put the slices of liver into the bag and shake it to coat them all over.

Heat the butter and oil in a large frying pan over the highest heat. Add the slices of liver – you will probably have to cook them in two goes – and cook them for not more than half a minute, which should make them browned on the outside and slightly pink inside. Transfer the liver to a heated serving dish, leaving the frying pan on the heat. Add the apple juice to the pan and bubble it fiercely for a minute, and then add the cream and bubble for another minute or so until thickened slightly. Remove the sauce from the heat, season it to taste and stir in the parsley. Pour the sauce over the slices of liver and serve at once.

MUSHROOMS STUFFED WITH VEAL AND TOMATOES

Preparation time: 15 minutes + 30 minutes baking   Serves 4

---

4 very large flat mushrooms

500 g (1 lb) minced veal

50 g (2 oz) fresh breadcrumbs

a small handful of finely sliced fresh basil or sage leaves

1 clove of garlic, chopped finely

2 medium-size firm tomatoes, cut into small pieces

a little olive oil

25 g (1 oz) grated parmesan cheese

salt and black pepper

Oven temperature:
Gas Mark 7/220°C/425°F

I associate veal almost entirely with Italy. It is certainly where I have enjoyed it more than anywhere else, partly because they cook it in such a variety of ways, but also because I think their rather older veal has a much better flavour. In England, however, I find minced veal very successful, especially when cooked with Italian flavourings. The Italians often stuff mushrooms with a breadcrumb mixture as a first course. Here, very large, flat mushrooms with a tasty veal stuffing, topped with parmesan, make an excellent main dish for lunch or supper. Serve these with a green salad and buttered noodles or mashed potato.

Preheat the oven. Cut the stalks out of the mushrooms and chop them finely. Put them into a mixing bowl with the minced veal, the breadcrumbs, the basil or sage leaves, the garlic and the tomatoes. Mix together well with a wooden spoon and season the stuffing generously with salt and black pepper. Smear the mushrooms on the outside with olive oil and put them, outside downwards, in a roasting pan. Divide the mixture roughly into four. Gather up each quarter, pat it roughly together and place it on top of one of the mushrooms. Lastly, top the mushrooms with the grated parmesan cheese.

Cook the mushrooms towards the top of the oven for 25–30 minutes until they are browned on top, and then transfer them to a warmed serving dish. Pour off the juices into a small saucepan, bring them to the boil and boil fiercely for a minute or two until they are reduced and syrupy. Spoon the juices over the mushrooms and serve at once.

Mushrooms Stuffed with Veal
and Tomatoes

Gnocchi Roulade Stuffed
with Broccoli and Mozzarella

Prawn Pasta

29

GNOCCHI ROULADE STUFFED WITH BROCCOLI AND MOZZARELLA

Preparation time: 40 minutes + 15 minutes baking   Serves 4

600 ml (1 pint) milk

125 g (4 oz) fine semolina

25 g (1 oz) butter

75 g (3 oz) grated cheese, such as strong Cheddar

2 egg yolks

¼ nutmeg, grated

500 g (1 lb) broccoli

1 large clove of garlic

2 tablespoons olive oil, plus extra for greasing

160 g (5½ oz) Italian mozzarella cheese

grated parmesan cheese

salt and black pepper

Oven temperature:
Gas Mark 9/240°C/475°F

I recently went back to Lerici, in Northern Italy, for the first time since I was about twelve. Surprisingly, it seemed to have changed very little; there were more white villas creeping up the hills overlooking the sea, but there was still the rather polite, old-fashioned atmosphere which I remembered. One thing I couldn't find was a little restaurant where I first tasted semolina gnocchi. Golden, light and cheesy, I found these irresistible, and I still do. In this recipe, the gnocchi mixture forms a roulade which is filled with crunchy pieces of broccoli and mozzarella cheese which oozes out and melts into strings. It is a delicious family supper dish, served with a juicy tomato salad, or one which you can also serve as a hot first course, in which case this quantity would serve six people.

Put the milk in a heavy saucepan and stir in the semolina. Bring it to the boil, stirring constantly and then simmer, still stirring, for 3−4 minutes until the mixture is very thick. Remove the pan from the heat and stir in the butter and grated cheese. Stir until melted. Then stir in the egg yolks and the nutmeg and season with salt and black pepper. Smear a large swiss roll tin or baking sheet (about 23 × 33 cm (9 × 13 inches) lightly with oil and spread the mixture evenly all over the bottom. Cover with a cloth and leave in a cool place until completely cold. Then chill in the fridge for 30 minutes or more.

Meanwhile, cut the thickest part of the stalk off the broccoli and chop the rest into very small pieces. Peel the garlic and chop it finely. Heat the oil in a large frying pan over a medium heat. Add the broccoli and cook it, stirring around frequently, for 8 minutes; add the chopped garlic and continue to stir over the heat for about another 2 minutes, or until the broccoli is just cooked but still slightly crunchy. Leave on one side to cool. Preheat the oven.

When the semolina mixture is chilled, slice the

mozzarella across thinly. Spread the broccoli all over the gnocchi and arrange three quarters of the mozzarella slices on top. Then, using your fingers, carefully and loosely roll up the gnocchi mixture like a swiss roll, enclosing the broccoli. Using a wide spatula and the palms of your hands transfer the roulade gently to an oiled, shallow ovenproof dish. Don't worry if it cracks a bit, you can always press it together again. Put the remaining slices of mozzarella on top and then sprinkle parmesan cheese generously all over the top. Put the roulade at the top of the oven for about 15 minutes until golden brown on top.

PRAWN PASTA

Preparation time: 30 minutes   Serves 4

1 large bulb of fennel

6 tablespoons virgin olive oil

4 cloves of garlic, cut into slivers

350 g (12 oz) pasta shells

1/4 – 1/2 nutmeg

250 g (8 oz) peeled prawns, thawed if frozen

salt and black pepper

To serve:

grated parmesan cheese (optional)

This is a simple dish of pasta and prawns with a sauce which combines some of my favourite Italian tastes: good olive oil, cooked fennel, garlic, and nutmeg. Even frozen prawns are enlivened by it, and fresh ones make a real treat, or you can use any other seafood.

Chop the fennel into small pieces, reserving any leafy bits. Put 3 tablespoons of the olive oil in a frying pan. Heat over a medium heat and add the chopped fennel. Fry gently for about 10 minutes, and then add the sliced garlic and cook for another 2–3 minutes. Remove from the heat and keep on one side. Bring a pan of salted water to the boil and add the pasta shells. While the pasta is cooking – it will take 12–15 minutes, depending on whether it is the fresh kind or not – grate the nutmeg into the frying pan of fennel and garlic. Add the remaining 3 tablespoons of olive oil and the prawns and season with a little salt and plenty of black pepper. Stir in any reserved fennel leaves. When the pasta has cooked, drain it and empty it into a heated serving bowl. If necessary, very gently re-heat the contents of the frying pan, and then turn it into the pasta, mixing well. Serve immediately, with grated parmesan cheese if you like.

PORK ROLLS STUFFED WITH ARTICHOKE, WITH MUSHROOM AND MUSTARD SAUCE

Preparation time: 20 minutes + 1¾ hours cooking   Serves 4

3 large globe artichokes

1 tablespoon lemon juice

1 clove of garlic, peeled and chopped roughly

8–10 black olives, stoned

4 thinly cut pork escalopes weighing about 350–500 g (12 oz–1 lb)

olive oil

caster sugar

300 ml (½ pint) milk

25 g (1 oz) butter

2 tablespoons cornflour

4 tablespoons whole-grain mustard

125 g (4 oz) button mushrooms, halved

salt and black pepper

Oven temperature:
Gas Mark 4/180°C/350°F

Although most of the wonderful bumper artichokes we buy in England are grown in Brittany, they are a vegetable which always reminds me of Italy. In Venice, in the early summer, one of the most beautiful sights is of boats laden down with a mountain of little purple and green artichokes making their way to the Rialto Market. This dish is made with large artichokes which are the ones we can usually buy here later in the summer, but their distinctive flavour is the same. Remember to drink some water while you are eating them; even city tap water will taste like a mountain spring! This is good accompanied by buttered egg noodles and broccoli.

Preheat the oven. Break the stems off the artichokes and boil them in salted water for 45 minutes or until the leaves come off easily. Put them into a sink of cold water to cool and after a few minutes twist out the centre leaves, revealing the hairy choke (diagram 1). Scrape out the choke and discard it (diagram 2). Remove them from the water, and, on a board, scrape the flesh off the remaining big leaves and put it in a food processor, adding lastly the delicious bottom of the artichoke. Add the lemon juice, the chopped garlic and the stoned olives and whizz to a purée. Season to taste with salt and black pepper and spread the paste on to the pork escalopes. Then roll the escalopes up gently and loosely like little swiss rolls and lay them in an open ovenproof dish, join-side down. Smear the rolls with olive oil, sprinkle them lightly with a little caster sugar and bake the dish in the centre of the oven for 1 hour.

Meanwhile, put the milk into a measuring jug. When the pork has cooked, pour the juices off into the measuring jug, with the milk. Put

Pork Rolls Stuffed with Artichokes, with Mushroom and Mustard Sauce

the rolls in a very low oven to keep warm. Melt the butter in a saucepan, remove from the heat and add the cornflour. Stir with a wooden spoon until smooth. Then stir in the milk and juices and the whole-grain mustard. Put the pan back on the heat, bring the sauce to the boil and let it bubble for 2–3 minutes. Add the button mushrooms and bubble it for another minute. Season to taste with salt and pepper and spoon over the rolls before serving.

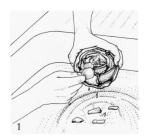

PORK BUNDLES STUFFED WITH BROCCOLI AND MOZZARELLA

Preparation time: 20 minutes + 50 minutes baking   Serves 4–5

500 g (1 lb) calabrese broccoli

160 g (5½ oz) Italian mozzarella cheese

1 clove of garlic, chopped finely

¼ nutmeg, grated

3 large eggs (size 1–2)

500 g (1 lb) pork fillet

olive oil

grated parmesan cheese

salt and black pepper

Oven temperature:
Gas Mark 4/180°C/350°F

It was in Italy, years ago, that I first tasted calabrese broccoli. This bright green broccoli with thick tender stems and full heads is now quite easy to find in shops all over England, but in those days the only broccoli we knew was the thin, leafy, sprouting broccoli and the more cauliflower-like purple-headed broccoli. But after the holiday in Italy I persuaded my father to grow the Italian variety in his Herefordshire garden, and it was a lovely treat among the carrots and cabbages.

I think these little bundles of soft pork fillet seem almost like a pasta made with meat. The pork fillet is hammered out to make a very thin, tender wrapping for the broccoli. The egg and mozzarella seep out during the cooking to form a delicious savoury custard in which the bundles are lightly set. I like serving it with a carrot purée and either buttered noodles or sauté potatoes.

Cut away the thickest part of the stem from the

34

broccoli and chop the rest up as small as you can. Put the broccoli into a mixing bowl. Cut the mozzarella up into small pieces and mix it with the broccoli. Add the garlic and the nutmeg and season with salt and black pepper. Whisk the eggs well and then stir them thoroughly into the broccoli mixture. Slice the pork fillet across into 5 mm (¼-inch) slices and lay them, spaced well apart, between two large oiled sheets of grease-proof paper; you will have to do this in batches. Bash the meat firmly between the sheets of paper, using a rolling pin or heavy, wide cleaver, until the pieces are very thin and about three times their original size. Preheat the oven.

Smear a large, shallow, ovenproof dish lightly with olive oil. Pile about a tablespoon of broccoli mixture on to each slice of pork and bring the meat up all round to enclose the filling roughly (the broccoli filling should still be partly visible). Lay the bundles closely in the dish, join side upwards. If there is any filling left over when you have finished all the bundles add some extra to those which look less bursting with it. Finally, spoon a very little olive oil over the bundles, together with a sprinkling of salt, pepper and a little grated parmesan cheese. Cook the bundles in the centre of the oven for 40–50 minutes until they are browned on top and surrounded by a set 'custard'.

PERA PALAS PIE

Preparation time: 1 hour + 30 minutes baking	Serves 6

1 large aubergine weighing about 350 g (12 oz)

lemon juice or white wine vinegar

3 tablespoons olive oil

25 g (1 oz) pine kernels, plus a few extra

500 g (1 lb) lean minced lamb

2 cloves of garlic, chopped finely

2 teaspoons paprika

a good handful of fresh chopped dill weed or 3 teaspoons dried dill weed

50 g (2 oz) plain flour

600 ml (1 pint) milk

250 g (8 oz) curd cheese

salt and black pepper

Oven temperature:
Gas Mark 5/190°C/375°F

When I first arrived in Turkey with a girlfriend at the age of eighteen, on a trip paid for by her generous father, we went to the Pera Palas Hotel in Istanbul, the legendary spies' hotel. It was certainly a hotel to capture our imagination, with its much faded grandeur: huge and shabby reception rooms, marble floored bathrooms and the ornate, gilded lift. The hotel was almost empty when we stayed there, and I shall always remember our first evening when the two of us sat completely alone in the dining room with a neat row of waiters staring at us curiously from the far end of the room.

Until that meal, I had always thought of dill weed as a Scandinavian herb and pine kernels as something characteristically Lebanese. In Istanbul, however, you will find fresh dill weed and pine kernels mixed with rice, lamb and fish. In this dish I have used them to make an exceptionally good type of moussaka with a Turkish flavour. The aubergine is surely to Turkey was the leek is to Wales and the smooth curd cheese topping of this dish is dotted with pieces of aubergine and toasted pine kernels. I serve it with rice and a green salad or vegetable and to make it more substantial I sometimes put a layer of sliced cooked potatoes between the meat and the topping.

Cut the unpeeled aubergine into 1 cm (½-inch) slices and smear them all over with the lemon juice or vinegar. Then rub the slices with salt and leave them in a colander in the sink for half an hour. Preheat the oven.

After half an hour, rinse the slices well, dry them with paper towels and cut them into small cubes. Heat 2 tablespoons of the olive oil in a large frying pan over a high heat, add the aubergines and stir them around for a few minutes until soft and browned. Transfer to a plate on one side. Now empty the 25 g (1 oz) pine kernels into the pan, stir them for a minute or two until browned and empty them on to another plate. Heat the remaining tablespoon of oil in the frying pan over a fairly high heat. Add the minced lamb and fry it, breaking the meat up, for a few minutes until any liquid has evaporated and the meat has browned. Add the chopped garlic and the paprika, cook for another minute or two and then remove the pan from the heat. Stir in the chopped dill weed and empty it into a shallow, ovenproof dish.

To make the topping, put the flour into a saucepan away from the heat and stir in a little of the milk with a wooden spoon until you have a smooth paste. Then stir in the remaining milk and bring it to the boil, stirring all the time, and let it bubble, still stirring, for 2–3 minutes. Then remove the pan from the heat, add the curd cheese and stir or whisk thoroughly until blended into the sauce. Season to taste with salt and pepper. Stir in the reserved fried aubergines and pine kernels and pour the sauce evenly over the lamb in the dish. Scatter a few more unfried pine kernels on top. Cook the pie towards the top of the oven for about 30 minutes until it has browned on top.

TURKISH PASTIES

Preparation time: 40 minutes + 20 minutes baking   Serves 4–5

For the filling:

300 g (10 oz) leeks
175 g (6 oz) potatoes
1 tablespoon olive oil
15 g (½ oz) butter
1 clove of garlic, chopped finely
2 teaspoons ground coriander
2 pinches of cayenne pepper
salt

In Turkey, you can find all sorts of 'börek' which are like tiny pasties made with crisp, paper-thin filo pastry. Some are filled with white cheese, some with meat, some with spinach. They are usually eaten as a snack or as an appetiser before a meal. These spiced leek and potato pasties are a little more substantial and can be eaten for lunch with a salad, or taken on a picnic, wrapped up to keep them warm. The pastry is a Turkish one made with yogurt and melted butter, quite a different type from filo but light and tasty.

Make the filling first. Wash the leeks and slice them across in thin rounds as far up the stalk as possible. Then chop the slices in half. Peel the

37

For the pastry:

125 g (4 oz) butter, plus
extra for greasing

1 tablespoon olive oil

1 small egg (size 5–6)

150 g (5.29 oz) carton of
natural yogurt

300 g (10 oz) plain flour,
plus extra for kneading

¼ teaspoon bicarbonate of
soda

1 teaspoon salt

1 egg yolk, beaten

Oven temperature:
Gas Mark 6/200°C/400°F

potatoes and cut them into very small cubes.
Heat the oil and butter in a largish frying pan
over a medium heat. Add the potatoes and cook,
stirring round now and then, for 5–7 minutes
until the potatoes are just tender. Then stir in the
chopped garlic, the coriander and the chopped
leeks. Cook, stirring often, for 2–3 minutes, just
until the leeks have softened. Season well with
salt and the cayenne pepper, remove from the
heat and leave until cold. Preheat the oven.

Melt the butter in a saucepan over a gentle heat
and leave on one side. Put the olive oil and egg
into a mixing bowl and whisk them lightly
together. Stir in the yogurt. Using a wooden
spoon stir the melted butter into the yogurt and
egg mixture, a little at a time. Sift the flour with
the bicarbonate of soda and the salt and then
gradually stir it into the yogurt and butter
mixture. Then knead the rather soft dough with
your hands on a floured surface for a few
minutes. Roll the dough to a thickness of 5 mm
(¼ inch), and, using a glass or sundae dish
10 cm (4 inches) in diameter, cut out circles from
the pastry. On to one side of each circle pile
about 2 teaspoons of filling; then fold over the
other side to form semicircular pasties and press
the edges to seal them. Re-roll the pastry as
necessary until the filling is used up. Lightly
grease a large baking sheet, lay the pasties on it
and brush them with beaten egg yolk. Cook just
above the centre of the oven for about 20 minutes
until golden brown.

MONKFISH KEBABS WITH AUBERGINE AND YOGURT SAUCE

Preparation time: 20 minutes + 30 minutes marinating   Serves 4

1 medium-size aubergine

750 g (1½ lb) filleted
monkfish

2 large bulbs of fennel

7 tablespoons olive oil

*Chicken kebabs, well seasoned, are often delicious, but
fish kebabs are my real favourite. Driving up the banks
of the Bosporus beyond Istanbul there are a string of
waterside restaurants and on a hot summer night they
are a wonderful escape from the turmoil and dirt of the
city. In one of these restaurants I had the ultimate fish
kebabs. They used swordfish – which I had seen*

juice of 1 large lemon

2 rounded teaspoons ground coriander

1 clove of garlic, peeled and chopped finely

240 g carton of Greek yogurt

2 tablespoons chopped fresh dill weed

salt and black pepper

earlier in the day in Istanbul market – staggeringly arranged, fanning outwards like silver catherine wheels. So these kebabs were literally swordfish served on a sword. Another firm-fleshed fish, monkfish, is an excellent alternative to swordfish. I serve the kebabs with brown rice and a salad.

First cut the unpeeled aubergine into 1 cm (½-inch) slices, rub the slices all over with salt and leave them in a colander in the sink for half an hour. Then cut the monkfish into 4–5 cm (1½–2-inch) chunks and cut the fennel into 5–7.5 cm (2–3-inch) pieces. Put 5 tablespoons of olive oil and the lemon juice into a mixing bowl, stir in the coriander and season with salt and black pepper. Add the pieces of fish and fennel and stir them around to coat them in the oil mixture. Leave in a cool place on one side.

After half an hour wash all the salt off the aubergine slices, pat them thoroughly dry with paper towels and cut them into 1 cm (½-inch) cubes. Now heat the remaining 2 tablespoons of olive oil in a frying pan over a medium heat, add the aubergine pieces and toss them around for a few minutes until they are browned on all sides and soft. Then add the chopped garlic, stir for another half a minute and put the pan one one side, off the heat. When the aubergine has cooled slightly, gently stir the yogurt in a mixing bowl until smooth, season it with salt and black pepper and then lightly stir in the aubergine, garlic and oil, lastly adding the chopped dill weed. Turn into a serving bowl and put aside.

Now thread the monkfish and fennel alternately on four to six long skewers, starting and finishing each skewer with a largish piece of fennel. Put the skewers under a very hot grill or on a barbecue grill, basting with any oil and lemon remaining in the bowl, for 5–7 minutes on each side, until the fish is blackened on the edges. Serve on or pushed off the skewers. Pour any cooking juices left in the grill over the top.

BOSPORUS MUSSEL STEW

Preparation time: 1 hour + 45 minutes cooking   Serves 6

500–625 g (1–1¼ lb)
aubergines

white wine vinegar

salt

1 kg (2 lb) fresh mussels

300 ml (½ pint) water

250 g (8 oz) small onions
(red ones if available), sliced
finely in rings

2 large cloves of garlic, sliced
finely

397 g (14 oz) can of
chopped tomatoes

2 tablespoons tomato purée

3 tablespoons olive oil

15 g (½ oz) pine kernels or
25 g (1 oz) blanched
almonds, split

2 heaped tablespoons
chopped fresh dill weed or
3 teaspoons dried dill weed

black pepper

When I was eighteen I travelled with a girlfriend on the old Orient Express from Paris to Istanbul. It was the last gasp of the famous train and there was no dining car. For three days we made do with cold snacks bought hurriedly off the platforms of stations on the way, but the discovery of Turkish food awaited us. For me, two ingredients epitomise meals I have eaten in Turkey over the years since my first visit; first and above all aubergines, and second the plump, orange-fleshed mussels of the Bosporus.

Cut the aubergines across in slices and then cut the slices in half, sprinkling them with the vinegar as you do so. Rub the slices all over with salt and put them in a colander to drain while you prepare the other ingredients.

Wash and scrub the mussels, discarding any that are open. Pour the water into a large saucepan and bring it to the boil. Add the mussels, cover them, and boil for about 2 minutes until all the shells have opened. Discard any that do not open. Pour the liquid from the mussels into a largish iron or other flameproof casserole. Extract the mussels from their shells and put them in a bowl on one side.

Rinse all the salt from the aubergines with

Bosporus Mussels Stew

40

running water. Bring the mussel liquid in the casserole up to the boil. Add the rinsed aubergines, the onions, the garlic, the canned tomatoes, the tomato purée, the olive oil and a generous sprinkling of black pepper. Stir together thoroughly, cover the dish and simmer it gently on top of the stove for about 45 minutes.

Check the dish for seasoning, though no added salt should be necessary. Add the mussels to the dish just to warm while you heat a small dry frying pan and toss the pine kernels or almonds in it for a minute or two to brown them. Just before serving, add them to the dish with the chopped dill weed and remove it from the heat. Serve with rice and either spinach or a green salad.

Monkfish Kebabs with Aubergine and Yogurt Sauce

Turkish Pasties

ATHENIAN PIE

Preparation time: 35 minutes + 45 minutes baking   Serves 8

250 g (8 oz) skinless
chicken breast fillets

500 g (1 lb) skinned cod fillet

125 g (4 oz) butter

1 large clove of garlic, peeled
and chopped finely

500 g (1 lb) ricotta, curd or
cottage cheese

4 large eggs (size 1–2)

2 teaspoons dried oregano

2 teaspoons dried chopped
dill weed or 1 tablespoon
chopped fresh dill weed

¼ nutmeg, grated

about 500 g (1 lb) filo pastry

salt and black pepper

Oven temperature:
Gas Mark 5/190°C/375°F

It was on Crete that I first saw filo pastry being made.
With his face and body white under a dusting of flour,
the town baker rolled the dough out with lightning
skill until he had a vast sheet as thin as tissue paper.
He then threw the whole sheet in the air, miraculously
not tearing it, swiftly folded it up like a newspaper, cut
it into oblong sheets and sold it to one of the customers
queueing at his door. It is this delicate, brittle pastry
which makes the large pies of Greece, which you find
in almost every small restaurant wherever you go, so
delectable. Luckily, it is now quite easy to buy
uncooked filo pastry in England and it can bring
exciting new possibilities to your kitchen repertoire.
There are endless variations on the crispy Greek pies
with fillings of cheese, spinach, fish, chicken or meat.
The following recipe is my version for a favourite
combination of mine: fish with chicken in a light,
herby cheese mixture. Everyone loves it, so it makes a
perfect and convenient family meal. It can be made
ahead and kept warm in the oven and needs only a
simple accompaniment of a green vegetable or just a
salad, although sometimes I serve it with a fresh
tomato sauce made by cooking chopped, peeled
tomatoes gently in butter until they turn to a sauce,
which should be seasoned with a little sugar, salt and
black pepper.

Preheat the oven. First prepare the filling. Cut the
chicken breasts across thinly and then cut them
into small pieces. Slice the fish into 2.5–5 cm
(1–2-inch) pieces. Heat 25 g (1 oz) of the butter
in a large, deep frying pan over a medium heat.
Add the chopped garlic and stir it round for a
minute and then add the chopped chicken,
stirring for 2 minutes until just sealed and white.
Then add the pieces of fish, distributing them
evenly. Cover the frying pan with a lid or foil
and cook for 4–5 minutes until the fish is just
cooked. Remove from the heat and leave in a
cool place until fairly cold.

Put the ricotta, curd or cottage cheese into a mixing bowl and whisk in the eggs, one at a time. Stir in the cooled chicken, fish and garlic mixture with any juices, add the herbs and nutmeg and season well with salt and pepper. Gently melt the remaining 75 g (3 oz) butter in a saucepan and then remove it from the heat. Brush some butter over the bottom and sides of an oblong ovenproof dish, with sides about 30 × 23 cm (12 × 9 inches). If you have one, an enamel dish will produce the best results because the pastry underneath will cook better.

Lay a sheet of filo pastry lengthways in the dish, overlapping the edges. Brush the pastry with more butter and lay another sheet across the dish, widthways this time and again over-lapping; in this way the sides of the dish are covered. Continue like this, brushing between each layer of pastry, for 8 layers. Then pour in the filling and smooth the surface. Bring the overlapping sheets over the top of the filling one at a time, brushing with butter between each layer. Then lay the remaining sheets of pastry on top – you will probably have to fold them in half – brushing with butter between each layer, and brushing the top sheet very generously.

Using a very sharp knife cut lines in the top layer of the pastry across the pie. Then cut more lines diagonally across to make a diamond pattern. Bake in the centre of the oven for about 45 minutes, until browned on top.

KIBRIZLI CAKE

Preparation time: 20 minutes + 45 minutes baking   Serves 8–10

For the cake:

butter for greasing

5 eggs

finely grated rind of 1 lemon

250 g (8 oz) caster sugar

125 g (4 oz) semolina

125 g (4 oz) ground almonds

a pinch of baking powder

150 ml (¼ pint) water

¼ teaspoon salt

1 tablespoon sesame seeds

For the syrup:

175 g (6 oz) granulated sugar

2 tablespoons clear or set honey

just under 300 ml (½ pint) water

juice of 1 lemon

Oven temperature:
Gas Mark 4/180°C/350°F

I have named this cake after the beautiful old house of a friend who lives in Istanbul on the Asian side of the Bosporus; we have had some magical meals in the waterfront garden of Kibrizli Yalisi. Turkish cakes are often made with semolina, almonds and honey and I devised this recipe to try and epitomise what the best of them can be like. It has turned out particularly well. You can either eat it with tea or coffee or as a pudding with yogurt.

Preheat the oven. Lightly butter a 20 cm (8–inch) deep cake tin (not one with a loose base) and line it with a disc of greaseproof paper. Break the egg whites into a large bowl and put the yolks into another. Add the grated lemon rind to the yolks, with the caster sugar. Whisk them until they are very pale and then add the semolina, the ground almonds, the baking powder and the water and whisk until smooth. Add the salt to the egg whites and whisk them until they stand in soft peaks. Then, using a metal spoon, fold them gently into the yolk mixture and pour it into the prepared cake tin. Sprinkle the sesame seeds gently over the top and then bake the cake in the centre of the oven for 40–45 minutes or until firm to the touch in the centre.

Meanwhile, make the syrup. Put the granulated sugar and honey into a saucepan, with the water. Dissolve over a low heat, and then increase the heat and boil fiercely for 4–5 minutes. Remove from the heat, pour in the lemon juice through a sieve and stir it in. Put the pan in a sink of cold water to cool.

When the cake is ready, remove it from the oven but leave it in its tin. Spoon the cold syrup gradually and evenly over the hot cake, letting it soak in. Leave the cake in the tin until cold and then loosen the sides carefully with a knife and turn it out (you may have to shake the tin). Turn the cake the right way up on to a serving plate.

Kibrizli Cake ▶
Walnut and Fruit Baklava

WALNUT AND FRUIT BAKLAVA

Preparation time: 25 minutes + 40 minutes baking
+ cooling   Serves 6–8

For the syrup:

150 g (5 oz) granulated
sugar

6 tablespoons water

1 tablespoon lemon juice

1 tablespoon rose-water or
orange-flower water

For the pastry:

125 g (4 oz) unsalted
butter, melted

250 g (8 oz) filo pastry

125 g (4 oz) walnuts,
chopped coarsely

1 tablespoon soft light
brown sugar

50 g (2 oz) sultanas

25 g (1 oz) currants

Oven temperatures:
Gas Mark 3/170°C/325°F
Gas Mark 7/220°C/425°F

*Most people are familiar with this Turkish or Greek
sweetmeat. Yet the baklava you can buy here, both in
continental grocers and in restaurants, is often
disappointing: stodgy and over-sweet, and rarely
made with butter. Now that it is possible to buy
ready-made filo pastry it is a dish which is well worth
making at home, as the result is so much better. I like
adding fruit and nuts and using a slightly sharp syrup.
Baklava with yogurt is an irresistible combination.
If you have any leftover pastry, wrap it well in the
plastic again and freeze it for another time. Rose-water
and orange-flower water are available from chemists.*

Make the syrup first. Dissolve the sugar in the
water and lemon juice over a low heat. Bring it
to the boil and boil fiercely for 2 minutes to
thicken it slightly. Remove it from the heat and
stir in the rose-water or orange-flower water.
Allow to cool and then leave the syrup in the
fridge. Preheat the oven to the lower setting.

To make the baklava, brush a large, rather
shallow, oblong dish or roasting tin, measuring
about 30 × 45 cm (12 × 18 inches), with some of
the melted butter. If your filo pastry is in very
large sheets, cut them in half and keep the rest
under a damp cloth until the moment you use
them. Lay one sheet on the bottom of the dish,
brush it with melted butter and continue in
layers until you have used up a little under half
the sheets, brushing with butter between each
layer and then folding over the edges if necessary
to fit the dish. Then evenly sprinkle over the
chopped nuts, the brown sugar, the sultanas and
the currants. Put on the remaining sheets of
pastry, again brushing with butter between each
and buttering the top piece as well. Then using a
sharp knife cut diagonal lines about 2.5 cm
(1 inch) apart across the pastry and then straight
lines lengthways, making diamond shapes,
without cutting right through.

Bake in the centre of the oven for 25–30 minutes and then raise the heat to the higher setting for another 8–10 minutes, or until the baklava is a rich golden brown. Remove from the oven and pour the cold syrup all over the baklava and then leave it to cool. To serve, cut the pastries out of the tray and arrange them in a pile on a serving dish.

FELIZ'S COURGETTE FRITTERS

Preparation time: 30 minutes   Serves 6

750 g (1½ lb) courgettes

2 cloves of garlic, chopped finely

a handful of finely chopped parsley

15–20 fresh mint leaves, chopped finely

2 teaspoons ground allspice

25 g (1 oz) grated parmesan cheese

1 egg, whisked lightly

about 6 tablespoons self-raising flour

groundnut oil for deep-frying

salt and black pepper

The shimmering city of Istanbul can also be greyer than the grimmest English day. On such a day, in pouring rain, I crossed the Bosporus by ferry to reach the Asian side to meet an unknown friend of a friend. It was bitterly cold and, having anticipated warm southern sun when I left England, I was quite inadequately dressed. With my bare, blue legs and sandals I sploshed through the puddles to a gloomy apartment building. Once inside I met Feliz and the day changed. The flat was warm and looked along the Bosporus towards the Sea of Marmara. She had cooked a delicious lunch for me and was full of ideas about what I should see, what I should eat and what I should cook when I returned to England. This simple and delicious recipe can be made very swiftly; the fritters are best eaten at once and make a nice first course with a bowl of yogurt as a sauce. Feliz says she also likes them cold.

Coarsely grate the unpeeled courgettes into a mixing bowl. Stir in the chopped garlic, the parsley and mint, the ground allspice, the grated parmesan cheese, salt and pepper and the whisked egg. Stir in the flour, which should be enough to bind the mixture thickly. Heat the groundnut oil in a large, deep frying pan until smoking. Drop tablespoons of the mixture into the oil. Shallow-fry the fritters for about 2 minutes on each side until golden brown, turning them once. When they look ready, remove them with a slotted spoon and drain them on absorbent kitchen paper towelling.

NURI BEY'S FRESH LEMON JELLY

Preparation time: 30 minutes + chilling overnight   Serves 6–8

150 g (5 oz) granulated
sugar

2–3 large sprigs of lemon
balm or mint

rind of 2 lemons, peeled off
in strips

1 litre (1¾ pints) water

75 g (3 oz) cornflour

juice of 6 lemons

To decorate:

walnut halves

This is a recipe I worked out years ago after a visit to Mr Bey's house in Istanbul. His cook was in fact Austrian, but she produced many excellent Turkish dishes and made use of all the local ingredients which she bought in the incomparable Istanbul food markets. This is not jelly as we know it; it can't be turned out of a mould and it certainly doesn't wobble. Instead it is smooth and opaque with a strong, sharp lemon flavour which makes it perfectly refreshing after a rich meal. Serve with creamed smatana, a delicious fermented milk, or cream.

Put the sugar, the lemon balm or mint leaves and the lemon peel into the water and boil them up together for 8–10 minutes. Remove the peel and leaves with a slotted spoon. Blend the cornflour with a little cold water to a smooth paste and then stir it into the hot lemon peel water. Bring the water to the boil, stirring all the time, and bubble it for a minute or two until thick. Stir in the juice of 3 lemons and boil for another 2 minutes; then leave it until cold and solid.

Add the juice of the other 3 lemons and whizz everything up in a food processor until smooth, or rub it through a sieve. Pour the jelly into a glass or china bowl and chill it well in the fridge overnight. Then decorate the top with walnut halves.

NORTH AFRICA

TIZI-N-TEST TAJINE

Preparation time: 25 minutes + 1½ hours cooking   Serves 6

1 kg (2 lb) lamb neck fillet
or lean lamb, cut into 5 cm
(2-inch) pieces

1 large red pepper, de-seeded
and cut into strips
lengthways

2 large cloves of garlic,
peeled and chopped roughly

5 cm (2-inch) piece of root
ginger, peeled and sliced
thinly

2 teaspoons ground
cinnamon

2 teaspoons paprika

50 g (2 oz) butter

about 900 ml (1½ pints)
water

350 g (12 oz) fresh okra

75–100 g (3–4 oz) whole
unskinned almonds

juice of 1 lemon

1 rounded tablespoon clear
or set honey

salt and black pepper

*The loveliest time to go to the south of Morocco is in
January or February when the almond blossom blooms
in the oasis on the desert side of the Atlas mountains.
On my first visit, a sort of belated honeymoon, there
was an excellent French-Moroccan restaurant on the
winding way up to the Tizi-n-Test mountain pass.
My husband, I discovered, had a terrible head for
heights, so we stopped for a tajine there to give him
courage for the alarming road ahead. The tajines, or
stews, of Morocco are easy to make. In England we
are not used to stews which look particularly beautiful,
but this lamb, okra and almond tajine is glossy, richly
coloured and tastes wonderful. Serve with either rice
or potatoes and a salad.*

Put the lamb into a large, heavy saucepan. Add
the pepper strips to the meat with the prepared
garlic, ginger, the spices and the butter. Season
with salt and black pepper and add the water,
which should just cover the meat. Cover the pan
and bring it to the boil; then lower the heat and
simmer gently for about 1½ hours until the
meat is meltingly tender.

Using a slotted spoon, transfer the meat,
pepper and slices of ginger to a heated, round
serving dish, leaving the liquid in the saucepan.
Cover the dish loosely with foil and keep it
warm in a very low oven. Cut the tops off the
okra and put them in a saucepan of boiling salted
water for about 3 minutes until just tender and
bright green. Drain and keep on one side. Add
the almonds, lemon juice and honey to the juices
in the saucepan. Bring them to the boil, stirring
to dissolve the honey. Then boil fiercely without
stirring for about 10 minutes until the sauce is
reduced and syrupy. Now mix the cooked okra
with the meat, spoon the sauce and almonds all
over the tajine and serve immediately.

EGYPTIAN PIZZA

Preparation time: 45 minutes
Serves 4–5

For the dough:

350 g (12 oz) plain flour, plus extra for rolling

½ teaspoon salt

300 ml (½ pint) boiling water

For the filling:

groundnut oil

250 g (8 oz) lean ground beef

1 teaspoon ground cinnamon

4–6 pinches of cayenne pepper

1 tablespoon tomato purée

40 g (1½ oz) butter

1 egg

125 g (4 oz) small onions (red ones if available), chopped small

a large handful of parsley, chopped roughly

sea salt

We had arrived late at night in Cairo and we were hungry. But no luck: all the restaurants were already closed. Suddenly, a mouthwatering smell enticed us down a dark side street. In a tiny shack between two high buildings a man was making what looked like a kind of layered pizza which people were taking away wrapped in newspaper. His hands worked like lightning, throwing the dough about and scattering on meat, spices and a whole egg before cooking the 'pizza' over extremely hot charcoal. We sat and ate at the only table while a little boy washed up at a sink beside us. These Egyptian 'pizzas' were wonderful. Since the cook worked so swiftly and spoke no English I could not be sure of how he did it, but I have used a Chinese pancake method and have recreated the Egyptian flavour from memory. Served with a green salad it makes a good supper dish, and my children love it. If you want a more fiery taste scatter on a finely chopped green chilli as well.

To make the dough, sift the flour and salt into a bowl and gradually pour in the boiling water, stirring with a wooden spoon until the mixture sticks together. Then gather it up and knead it with the palms of your hands on a flat surface for a few minutes until the dough is smooth and elastic. Cover it with cling film and leave it for 30 minutes or more but do not chill. Meanwhile, heat 1 tablespoon of groundnut oil in a frying pan over a high heat. Add the ground beef and stir it around, digging with a spoon to break it up. Add the ground cinnamon and the cayenne pepper and stir the beef for 4–5 minutes until browned. Then stir in the tomato purée, remove the pan from the heat and leave it to cool.

Melt the butter in a saucepan and put it on one side. Break the egg into a bowl and whisk it lightly with a fork. Now roll the ball of dough out on a floured surface into a large circular shape 45–50 cm (18–20 inches) in diameter. Brush it all over with the melted butter and then

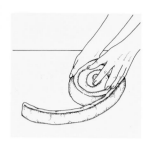

evenly scatter on the cooked meat, the chopped onion and the parsley, and sprinkle it lightly with sea salt. Pour the egg roughly over the centre and roll up the pancake, making a long, flattish roll. Now carefully fold over the roll into a spiral to form a sort of wheel (as in the diagram). Using plenty of flour, roll out the circle into a large pancake 25–28 cm (10–11 inches) in diameter and 1–2 cm (½–¾-inch) thick. If you have a very big frying pan roll the pancake slightly wider.

Heat a film of groundnut oil in a large frying pan over a medium heat. Carefully transfer the pancake to the pan and fry it for a few minutes until it is rich brown underneath. The easiest way to turn it is with a wide spatula and an oven glove, literally lifting it up and over. Fry the other side and then turn it on to a serving plate and serve at once.

CHICKEN STUFFED WITH COUSCOUS

Preparation time: 30 minutes + 1¼ hours cooking

Serves 4–5

75 g (3 oz) couscous
50 g (2 oz) butter
1 clove of garlic, peeled and chopped finely
40 g (1½ oz) blanched whole almonds
2 teaspoons ground cinnamon
1 teaspoon whole cumin seeds
25 g (1 oz) seedless raisins
1.5 kg (3 lb) maize-fed chicken
2 teaspoons paprika
2 tablespoons olive oil
2 teaspoons clear or set honey
1 tablespoon lemon juice
1 tablespoon tomato purée
150 ml (¼ pint) water
salt and black pepper

Oven temperature:
Gas Mark 6/200°C/400°F

Couscous is eaten all over North Africa. It doesn't look very inspiring, rather like cracked wheat, but subtly spiced and studded with almonds and dried fruit it tastes delicious. In Morocco couscous is used to stuff pigeons and chickens; it makes a delicious stuffing, very light in texture, and it can be a nice change from the more usual stuffed and roasted chicken.

Put the couscous in a bowl. Pour in plenty of hot water, soak for about 10 minutes until it is puffed up and then drain it in a sieve. Melt the butter in a medium-sized saucepan over a low heat, add the chopped garlic and the almonds and stir over a low heat for about 2 minutes. Add the cinnamon and cumin seeds and stir for another minute. Add the drained couscous and the raisins and season with salt and black pepper. Cover the pan and continue cooking over a low heat for about another 8 minutes.

Meanwhile, preheat the oven. Leave the couscous to cool slightly and then spoon it into the body cavity of the chicken, pressing it in. Mix the paprika with the olive oil and smear it all over the chicken. Put the chicken in a roasting pan and cook in the centre of the oven for 1–1¼ hours.

When cooked, remove the chicken to a carving board. Pour any excess fat from the pan and stir the honey, lemon juice, tomato purée and water into the pan juice. Bubble everything together on top of the stove, stirring for a minute or two. Season to taste with salt and pepper and then pour into a gravy jug to serve with the chicken.

Chicken Stuffed with Couscous

Tizi-n-Test Tajine

Egyptian Pizza

THE MIDDLE EAST

DREAM OF DAMASCUS

Preparation time: 30 minutes marinating + 40 minutes + 55 minutes cooking   Serves 4

250 g (8 oz) skinless chicken breast fillets

3 tablespoons lemon juice

2 tablespoons olive oil

1 tablespoon fresh chopped mint leaves

125 g (4 oz) bulghur (cracked wheat)

500 g (1 lb) lean minced lamb

2 teaspoons ground coriander

1 teaspoon ground cumin

2 cloves of garlic, peeled and chopped roughly

3–4 pinches of cayenne pepper

1 tablespoon tomato purée

plain flour

sunflower oil

2 × 240 g cartons of Greek yogurt

2 teaspoons cornflour

1 tablespoon water

salt and black pepper

Oven temperature:
Gas Mark 5/190°C/375°F

Children nearly always love meatballs and as a child in Syria I had the opportunity to try an enormous variety of them. The ones I liked best were the kibbeh: a mixture of pounded lamb and cracked wheat, which were often stuffed and either fried, stewed in a sauce or even eaten raw. I make a spicy kibbeh mixture into larger balls than usual, which I stuff with a luscious centre of marinated chicken breast. The balls are cooked in a thick yogurt sauce and the result is universally popular. Even my vegetarian daughter, who adores anything made with cracked wheat, looks at it rather longingly when I put it on the table. I serve my kibbeh with long-grain rice and a mixed salad. If you have any pine kernels, toss a handful of them in a dry, hot frying pan for a minute or two to brown them and then scatter them over the meatballs before serving.

Chop the chicken fillets into smallish pieces. Into a fairly shallow dish or bowl put the lemon juice, the olive oil, a good sprinkling of black pepper and the chopped mint. Stir in the chopped chicken, cover the container and leave it to marinate at room temperature for at least half an hour. Leave the cracked wheat to soak in a bowl of water. Preheat the oven.

When the chicken has marinated, drain the cracked wheat thoroughly. Put the minced lamb into a food processor with the ground spices, the chopped garlic, some cayenne pepper, the tomato purée and a sprinkling of salt. Whizz until the meat is pasty. Add the drained, cracked wheat and whizz until it is evenly mixed. Divide the mixture into eight pieces, form them into balls and then flatten into circles like wide, fairly thin hamburgers. Spoon the marinated chicken into even piles in the middle of each flattened piece of lamb mixture and then carefully draw up the sides in order to enclose the chicken, cupping it gently in your hands to form a ball and pressing together any cracks which may appear. Put some plain flour into a mixing bowl and put the meatballs into it one at a time to coat them generously with flour. Pour about 5 mm (¼ inch) sunflower oil into a large frying pan and put over a high heat until it smokes. Then gently add the meatballs and fry them, turning them carefully with a spatula just until they are browned all over. Transfer the meatballs with a slotted spatula to an ovenproof dish, not too shallow, in which they will fit in one layer.

Put the yogurt into a saucepan. Mix the cornflour in a cup with the water and stir it into the yogurt with a little salt. Bring to the boil, stirring all the time with a wooden spoon in one direction only. Then turn down the heat and let the mixture only just bubble in the open pan for 10 minutes. Season with a little cayenne pepper. Then pour the yogurt sauce into the dish with the meatballs, trying to pour it in between them rather than on top. Cover with foil or a lid. Put the dish in the centre of the oven and bake for 50–55 minutes.

CHICKEN FIRUZABAD WITH FLUFFY RICE

Preparation time: 1 hour soaking + 30 minutes   Serves 4
+ 40 minutes cooking

250 g (8 oz) basmati rice

2 tablespoons salt

50 g (2 oz) butter

1 tablespoon olive oil

1 large onion, cut up fairly small

4 chicken breast joints

75 g (3 oz) dried apricots, halved

50 g (2 oz) pitted prunes, halved

50 g (2 oz) unblanched almonds (in their skins)

1 teaspoon ground cinnamon

600 ml (1 pint) water

salt and black pepper

Years ago, newly married, my husband and I went on an exciting journey through Iran, which we then thought of as Persia. Years and years before us, Robert Byron had travelled there and written a wonderful book called 'The Road to Oxiana'. Several times we tried to retrace his footsteps exactly and one day we really felt that we were seeing the country as he had seen it, even though we were in a car and he had been on horseback. This was the day we went to a village called Firuzabad, which is near Shiraz, in the south. Nothing seemed to have changed since Robert Byron's visit, and there were nomad families camping near the ruined mosque. After a wonderful day we were invited to eat in the big house of the village. The meal was delectable; a typical Persian dish of chicken cooked with dried fruits and fluffy 'chillau' rice. I am still convinced that it is the best rice in the world, and I am grateful to Claudia Roden for teaching me how to cook basmati rice in the Persian way, and so bring back the memory of it. I accompany this luscious dish simply with a green salad.

At least an hour before you begin cooking the chicken, wash the rice very thoroughly by putting it in a sieve and rinsing it through. Put the rice in a bowl, add 2 tablespoons of salt, cover with warm water and leave on one side to soak.

To prepare the chicken, in a large iron or other flameproof casserole melt 25 g (1 oz) of the butter with the olive oil, over a medium heat. Add the onion and cook it for several minutes until soft, stirring often. Then, using a slotted spoon, remove the onion and put it in a bowl or on a plate on one side. Turn up the heat under the casserole slightly and add the chicken joints. Fry them on each side to seal and brown them well. Then return the onions to the dish, together

Chicken Firuzabad with Fluffy Rice

with the prepared apricots, the prunes and the almonds. Sprinkle on the cinnamon and season with salt and black pepper. Pour in the water. Cover the dish, bring to the boil and then simmer very gently for 30–40 minutes, until the chicken is tender.

Meanwhile, put a fairly large saucepan full of well salted water on to the heat and bring it to the boil. Drain the soaked rice, add it to the boiling water and boil it briskly for 4–6 minutes; the rice should still be slightly underdone. Drain the rice, rinse it and leave it on one side.

When the chicken is cooked, lift out the joints with a slotted spatula and put them on a plate on one side. Then boil up the juices and fruit fiercely in the open dish for a few minutes, stirring two or three times to prevent sticking, until the sauce is reduced and very thick and syrupy. Spoon on to the plate with the chicken pieces and wash out and dry the casserole dish. Then melt the remaining 25 g (1 oz) of butter gently in the clean casserole, put in the drained rice and arrange the chicken joints on top, spooning the thick sauce over each joint as you do so. Cover the casserole with a tea towel, put the lid tightly over the top and bring the corners of the cloth up over the lid to keep them from burning on the heat. Cook over the lowest possible heat for 20–25 minutes until the rice is fluffy and tender.

BULGHUR FLAN WITH PINE KERNELS

Preparation time: 45 minutes soaking + 15 minutes   Serves 6
+ 45 minutes baking

175 g (6 oz) bulghur
(cracked wheat)

500 g (1 lb) lean minced
lamb

1 medium-size onion,
chopped finely

a handful of mint leaves,
chopped

2 teaspoons ground cumin

1 egg, whisked

1 clove of garlic

25 g (1 oz) pine kernels

salt and black pepper

Oven temperature:
Gas Mark 4/180°C/350°F

When I lived in Syria as a child, a regular Sunday outing used to be to drive over the border into the Lebanon and have a picnic in some pine woods. As a result I associate pine kernels more than anything with Lebanese food, although they are used all over the Middle East. Bulghur (cracked wheat) is another Lebanese favourite, and this combination of cracked wheat and lamb, enhanced by cumin and mint and topped with golden pine kernels, was one of my favourite tastes when I lived in that part of the world. This is an easy dish to make and I find it very useful for family lunches, accompanied by a salad and some yogurt and chopped cucumber to spoon on as a sauce.

Soak the cracked wheat in a bowl of water for 30–45 minutes. Preheat the oven. Drain and squeeze it dry and put it into a mixing bowl with the minced lamb, the chopped onion, the chopped mint leaves and the cumin. Season generously with salt and black pepper and mix together thoroughly with a wooden spoon. Then mix in the whisked egg. Turn the mixture into a 25 cm (10-inch) earthenware flan dish and press it down evenly. Peel the garlic and slice it across as finely as possible. Scatter the slivers of garlic and the pine kernels on top of the meat mixture, pressing them down a bit with the flat of your hand. Put the flan towards the top of the oven for about 45 minutes until well browned on top. Serve cut in slices like a normal flan.

LAMB MEATBALLS POACHED IN TOMATO AND CHICK-PEA SAUCE

Preparation time: 20 minutes + 30 minutes cooking   Serves 4

500 g (1 lb) minced lamb

4 cloves of garlic

grated rind and juice of 1 lemon

1 teaspoon ground cumin

2 teaspoons ground cinnamon

a large handful of fresh mint leaves, chopped finely

25 g (1 oz) fresh breadcrumbs

oil for frying

397 g (14 oz) can of chopped tomatoes

1 tablespoon tomato purée

432 g (15¼ oz) can of chick-peas, drained

1 teaspoon crushed coriander seeds

salt and black pepper

I am never tired of the endless variety of meatballs found all over the Middle East. When I arrived in Syria at the age of seven I immediately took to them, and now I only have to throw together some lamb, fresh mint and spices, and the sights and smells of my childhood in Damascus are brought back to me.

Put the lamb in a bowl. Peel and chop two cloves of garlic finely and add them to the lamb, with the grated lemon rind, the ground cumin and cinnamon, the chopped mint leaves and the breadcrumbs. Season with salt and plenty of black pepper and mix thoroughly together with a wooden spoon. Using damp hands, form the mixture into walnut-sized balls. Heat a little oil in a frying pan, and fry the balls over a fairly high heat just to brown them all over. Remove from the heat and put the balls on some absorbent kitchen paper towelling.

Empty the chopped tomatoes into an iron or other flameproof casserole, stir in the tomato purée and the lemon juice and add the drained chick-peas. Season with black pepper and a little salt. Put in the fried meatballs. Cover the casserole and bring it to the boil over a high heat; then turn the heat down to as low as possible and cook it for 30 minutes. Lastly, peel the remaining two cloves of garlic, cut them in half and slice them thinly. Heat a very little oil in a frying pan over a fairly high heat. Add the garlic and the crushed coriander seeds and toss around until they are dark brown. Scatter on top of the meatballs and sauce before serving.

Bulghur Flan with Pine Kernels
Lamb Meatballs Poached in Tomato and Chick-pea Sauce

SOUTH EAST ASIA

STUFFED TURKEY BREASTS IN CHINESE PASTIES

Preparation time: 1 hour + 2 hours resting + 25 minutes cooking

Serves 4

75 g (3 oz) plain flour, plus extra for kneading

75 g (3 oz) strong white flour

½ teaspoon salt

175 ml (6 fl oz) boiling water

4 boneless turkey breast steaks weighing about 750 g (1½ lb)

2 cloves of garlic

2.5 cm (1-inch) piece of fresh ginger

125 g (4 oz) fresh beansprouts

1 teaspoon ground coriander

1 teaspoon mustard seeds

3 tablespoons oyster sauce

oil for greasing

To serve:

lettuce leaves

soy sauce

From the outside this looks like a steamed Cornish pasty, but the enticing smell tells you immediately it has Far Eastern connections. The turkey breast is stuffed with beansprouts and flavoured with oyster sauce, and this is a good dish for anyone trying to follow a low-fat diet.

Sift the flours and salt into a bowl. Stir in the boiling water with a wooden spoon until the dough sticks together. Knead it with the palm of your hand on a floured surface until the dough is smooth and elastic. Wrap the ball of dough in cling film and leave to rest for 1½–2 hours.

Meanwhile, prepare the filling. Using a very sharp knife, carefully cut a deep pocket in the turkey steaks. Peel the garlic and ginger and chop them together very finely. Put the beansprouts in a bowl and add the chopped garlic and ginger, the ground coriander, the mustard seeds and 1 tablespoon of oyster sauce. Spoon the beansprout mixture into the cavities in the turkey breasts, pressing it in.

When the dough has rested, divide it into four pieces and roll these into four balls. Roll out one ball fairly thinly on a floured surface to a circular shape. Place a stuffed turkey breast on one side of the circle, moisten the edge on one side of the circle and bring the pastry over to enclose the piece of turkey and make a semicircular shape like a pasty. Press the edges to seal. Repeat the process with the other three balls of pastry.

Brush the remaining 2 tablespoons of oyster sauce on both sides of the pasties and place them on an oiled steaming tray or trays. (If your steamer is small you may have to cook the pasties in two batches, and keep the first lot

warm in a covered dish in a low oven.) Steam the
pasties for 20–25 minutes. Lift the pasties
carefully out of the steamer with a spatula and
put them in a warmed serving dish on a bed of
lettuce leaves. Just before putting them on the
table, sprinkle on a little soy sauce.

CITRUS SPICED SPARE RIBS

Preparation time: 10 minutes + 1¾ hours cooking   Serves 4–5

1.5 kg (3 lb) spare ribs

2.5 cm (1-inch) piece of root
ginger

2 cloves of garlic

1 orange

1 lemon

2 rounded teaspoons ground
coriander

¼–½ teaspoon cayenne
pepper

3 tablespoons clear or set
honey

3 tablespoons tomato
ketchup

1 tablespoon sunflower oil

salt

Oven temperatures:
Gas Mark 4/180°C/350°F
Gas Mark 6/200°C/400°F

*Originating in the East, spare ribs have become one of
the most universal dishes there are, and they are
universally popular with both adults and children as
well. There are countless recipes for cooking spare
ribs, but most of them produce rich, spicy ribs, glazed
with the honey or sugar in the marinade with which
they are coated before cooking. I cannot decide where I
have tasted the most memorable spare ribs but I
particularly like this rather tangy version which fills
our kitchen with an aromatic, mouthwatering smell
while the ribs are cooking. I like serving them with a
casserole of brown rice cooked with chopped peppers
and tomatoes, and a crisp, green salad.*

Preheat the oven to the lower setting. Put the
spare ribs in a roasting pan, cover it with foil and
cook in the centre of the oven for 30 minutes.

Meanwhile, peel the ginger and the garlic and
chop them up roughly. Cut the unpeeled orange
and lemon in quarters and extract any pips. Put
into a food processor with the chopped ginger
and garlic, the coriander and cayenne pepper,
the honey, the tomato ketchup and sunflower
oil. Season with salt. Whizz thoroughly until as
smooth as possible. Remove the spare ribs from
the oven and pour off all the liquid. Turn the
oven up to the second setting. Pour the sauce
from the food processor all over the spare ribs
and turn them in it to make sure they are coated
all over. Then cook towards the top of the oven
for 1–1¼ hours until rich golden brown all
over, basting now and then and turning the ribs
over half-way through the cooking.

ECHOES OF BETUTU DUCK

Preparation time: 20 minutes + 1 hour marinating
+ 7 hours cooking + 10 minutes   Serves 8

2–2.25 kg (4½–5 lb) duck

6 hard-boiled eggs, peeled

For the marinade:

1 tablespoon tamarind
concentrate or 2 tablespoons
lemon juice

3 tablespoons groundnut oil·

2 tablespoons soy sauce

2 tablespoons oyster sauce

2 heaped tablespoons soft
light brown sugar

5 cm (2-inch) piece of root
ginger

3 cloves of garlic

3 fresh bay leaves

2 rounded teaspoons
coriander seeds

3 fresh green chillies,
de-seeded and cut up roughly

To serve:

a large handful of fresh
coriander leaves

Oven temperature:
Gas Mark ½/130°C/250°F

*Betutu duck is a special dish from the hills of Bali
which is traditionally cooked by a local priest. He rubs
the duck with sauce and spices, wraps it in a large
betel-nut leaf and buries it underground, under a layer
of smouldering rice husks, for up to 24 hours. Some of
the Balinese spices are impossible to find here and of
course the method of cooking cannot be imitated, but
the duck that the priest cooked for us in Bali was so
meltingly delicious that I resolved to emulate it as best
I could. I am pleased with the result. It is unusual, and
a good way to make one duck feed a lot of people.
Remember to start well in advance as it takes a long
time to cook. Serve with basmati rice and a mixed
green salad.*

Put all the marinade ingredients into a food
processor and whizz until the mixture is as
smooth as possible. Put a tablespoon of the
marinade mixture as far inside the duck's body
cavity as possible and another spoonful in the
centre. Put in the whole eggs and finally spoon
in a third tablespoon of the marinade. Spread out
a double layer of large sheets of greaseproof
paper. Put the duck in the centre, and, using a
very sharp knife, cut eight long incisions along
the breast of the duck. Spoon on the remaining
marinade, rubbing it well into the duck all over
with your hands. Enclose the duck in the greaseproof paper and then in a double layer of foil.
Leave at room temperature for an hour or more
before cooking.

Preheat the oven. Then put the packaged duck
into a roasting pan and cook in the centre of the
oven for 6–7 hours.

During the cooking, the duck fat will seep out
into the pan: at the end, pour it off into a bowl
and keep it for when you next roast potatoes.
Open the package and pour off the brown juices

Echoes of Betutu Duck

into a saucepan. The duck will look in a sorry state, but don't worry! Pull the very soft flesh off with a fork and pile it on a large, shallow, warmed serving dish. Cut the eggs in half and arrange them, yolk-side up, round the duck flesh. Boil the juices up over the fiercest heat for 5 minutes or more until well reduced and thickened. Pour this sauce over the duck flesh. Chop the coriander leaves roughly, sprinkle them all over the dish and mix in slightly with the duck.

STUFFED STICKY RICE ROLLS

Preparation time: 1 hour + chilling   Serves 6–8

250 g (8 oz) glutinous rice

a little under 450 ml (¾ pint) salted water

175 g (6 oz) skinned chicken breast fillets

1 fresh green chilli

2.5 cm (1-inch) piece of root ginger, peeled

1 tablespoon sunflower or groundnut oil, plus extra for greasing

1 tablespoon soy sauce

a medium-size head of chinese leaves

salt

To serve:

more soy sauce

When I was bumping through Java on a bus, increasingly hot and sticky, I used to revive myself with the little snacks bought from roadside stalls wherever we stopped on the way. Far Eastern 'finger foods' can be excellent. A lot of them, mostly sweet but some savoury, were made with sticky rice, as its stickiness makes it so convenient to wrap up, stuff and eat in your fingers and it has a particular texture which I love. I really prefer it in savoury dishes, so I made these cold rolls stuffed with spicy chicken breast which can be eaten as part of a cold lunch or as a first course, or be taken on a picnic, or even a bus ride!

Put the rice in a sieve and wash it thoroughly with running water. Then put it in a bowl with unsalted water to cover and soak for at least 30 minutes. Turn the rice into a sieve and rinse it through again with plenty of running water. Put the rice into a saucepan, add the salted water, cover the pan and put it over a high heat. When the water has come to the boil, lower the heat to as low as possible and continue cooking in the covered pan for 20–30 minutes until the rice has absorbed all the water and is softly stuck together.

Meanwhile, prepare the other ingredients. Cut the chicken breast fillets into very small pieces. Cut open the chilli under water, remove the seeds and then chop it finely, with the ginger.

Heat the oil in a pan over a medium heat. Add the chicken and stir it around, and then add the ginger and chilli and stir constantly for 2–3 minutes until the chicken is cooked. Then add the soy sauce and stir, coating the chicken pieces, for another half a minute or so. Remove the pan from the heat. Detach the whole, large chinese leaves. Bring a large pan of salted water to the boil. Plunge in the leaves, cover the pan and boil for about 5 minutes until soft. Drain in a colander and rinse with cold water to cool. Turn on to a towel, put another towel on top and pat dry thoroughly.

When the sticky rice is cool enough to handle, oil a large baking sheet or flat surface and press the rice out in two long strips about 6.5 cm (2½ inches) wide. Spoon the chicken mixture lengthways down the centre of each strip (diagram 1). Then bring up the sides of the strip and press them together to enclose the chicken filling (diagram 2). Cut the strips across at 5 cm (2-inch) intervals. Carefully take up these rolls, roll them up fairly loosely in the limp chinese leaves and place the rolls join-side down on a serving dish. Leave until completely cold and then cover the dish with cling film and refrigerate if you are keeping them before eating. Just before serving, sprinkle a trickle of soy sauce over the rolls.

 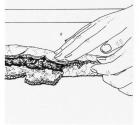

PRAWNS AND BRIGHT VEGETABLES IN COCONUT MILK

Preparation time: 45 minutes   Serves 4

1 teaspoon star anise

75 g (3 oz) block of creamed coconut

1 teaspoon salt

600 ml (1 pint) boiling water

2 tablespoons sunflower oil

2 large cloves of garlic, chopped finely

2 medium-size red peppers, de-seeded and sliced thinly

2.5 cm (1-inch) piece of root ginger, cut into small thin strips

125 g (4 oz) whole baby corn, fresh if possible, or canned

2 medium-size avocados

250 g (8 oz) peeled prawns, thawed if frozen

1 small cos lettuce, sliced at 1 cm (½-inch) intervals

salt and cayenne pepper

What I like best about much Chinese and Far Eastern food is that most of the ingredients are either raw or hardly cooked at all. In this way no vitamins are lost or textures destroyed and the dish tastes wonderfully fresh as it comes straight from stove to table. When entertaining, many of us who cook at home with no help feel that in order to avoid panic and muddle at the last moment we must stick to dishes which can be prepared well ahead and either re-heated or kept warm. Though you might be surprised, this dish, despite its Far Eastern feel, can be prepared ahead, leaving you with only a few minutes simple cooking just before you eat. Everything up until the cooking of the peppers and the addition of the coconut milk can be done in advance. All you have to do just before your meal is to bring the coconut milk up to the boil and add the corn and your prepared ingredients; it will be ready to eat in no more than five minutes. This lovely dish, which I serve simply with rice or creamy white rice-noodles, is similar to many I had in Indonesia with, as I often found in that country, a slight Chinese influence.

Grind the star anise in a coffee grinder or with a pestle and mortar. Break the creamed coconut up roughly, put it into a measuring jug with 1 teaspoon salt, pour over the boiling water and stir until the coconut cream has dissolved. Then put the sunflower oil in a wok or large iron or other flameproof casserole over a medium heat. Add the ground star anise, the chopped garlic, the sliced peppers and the ginger. Stir around for a moment and then cover the wok or casserole and cook over a low heat for 10–15 minutes, stirring often, until the peppers are soft. Then add the coconut milk, and if you are making this in advance, leave on one side.

Stuffed Sticky Rice Rolls
Prawns and Bright Vegetables in Coconut Milk

When you are ready to eat, bring the mixture to the boil and add the baby corn. Cover the pan and simmer for 5 minutes. Test for seasoning; add a little salt and cayenne pepper if necessary. Then cut the avocados in half, extract the stone, peel the halves and cut in half-moon slices. Add them to the coconut milk mixture with the prawns and sliced lettuce. Cover the pan again and remove from the heat after half a minute. Turn into a heated serving dish and serve .

BALINESE CARROT CAKE

Preparation time: 15 minutes + 1¾ hours baking   Serves 8

175 g (6 oz) caster sugar

2 rounded tablespoons clear honey

250 ml (8 fl oz) sunflower oil, plus extra for greasing

3 large eggs (size 1–2)

1 teaspoon ground cardamom

½ teaspoon salt

175 g (6 oz) self-raising wholemeal or 81% flour or plain wholemeal flour plus 1½ teaspoons baking powder

300 g (10 oz) carrots, grated

125 g (4 oz) unsweetened desiccated coconut

125 g (4 oz) walnuts, chopped roughly

Oven temperature:
Gas Mark 4/180°C/350°F

Some time ago my husband came back from America bringing me a slice of a carrot cake which had been cooked for his birthday in a small town in Kentucky. Ever since then I have loved carrot cake, and have tried many of the countless recipes for it. The last place I had expected to find this favourite cake was in Indonesia! However, in the hills of Bali, a small teahouse made a carrot cake with coconut spiced with cardamom and to me it is the best of all. You can sandwich the cake with a layer of sweetened cream cheese, but it is so moist that I prefer it plain.

Preheat the oven. Grease an 18–20 cm (7–8-inch) cake tin (not one with a loose base) and line it with a disc of greaseproof paper. Put the caster sugar and the honey into a mixing bowl. Add the sunflower oil and whisk until well mixed. Whisk in the eggs one at a time until amalgamated, and then continue whisking until the mixture is pale and frothy. Mix the ground cardamom and salt into the flour and then whisk the flour into the egg mixture a little at a time until thoroughly mixed. Stir in the grated carrots, the coconut and the chopped walnuts and pour the mixture into the prepared cake tin. Cook in the centre of the oven for 1½–1¾ hours until a small, sharp knife stuck into the centre comes out clean. If the top of the cake begins to look too brown before it is cooked, lay a piece of greaseproof paper or foil loosely on it.

CHILLI AND PEANUT PORK KEBABS

Preparation time: 20 minutes + 2−3 hours marinating   Serves 4−5

750 g (1½ lb) boneless pork shoulder steaks or boneless chicken

2 green chillies

2 cloves of garlic, peeled

3 rounded tablespoons smooth peanut butter

2 teaspoons tamarind concentrate (optional) or 4 teaspoons lemon juice

3 tablespoons groundnut or sunflower oil

1 level tablespoon black treacle

1 rounded teaspoon ground coriander

2 medium-size red peppers

salt

The marinade for these kebabs is more or less Indonesian in character. My travelling companion through Java was a vegetarian, and even to me an expedition to the meat markets was slightly off-putting. Under a dark cover in steaming heat unidentifiable bits of animal were piled up. On restaurant menus chicken's neck, dried lung and 'fried cows soft part' were as commonplace as steak or chops are to us. On the street stalls, however, tiny kebabs of meat and chicken, normally served with a peanut sauce, were delicious. I use a peanut sauce to marinate pieces of pork or boneless chicken, which makes them tender and tasty. The kebabs can be grilled on a barbecue in summer and are also delicious cooked ahead to eat cold on a picnic. If serving hot, have them with rice and a bowl of yogurt to use as a sauce.

Cut the pork or chicken into roughly 2.5 cm (1-inch) cubes and put these in a bowl. Cut the chillies open under running water and remove the seeds. Chop the garlic and chillies together very finely. In a smaller bowl, put the peanut butter, the tamarind concentrate, the oil, the treacle, the coriander and the chopped chilli and garlic. Stir to mix thoroughly and season with salt. Turn into the bowl of pork or chicken and stir with a wooden spoon to coat the meat all over with the paste. Cover the bowl, and leave it for 2−3 hours at room temperature.

Then cut the red peppers open, discard the seeds and cut the peppers into roughly 2.5 cm (1-inch) pieces. On long skewers, thread pieces of meat, alternating them with pieces of red pepper, and lay the skewers on a grill. Cook under a hot grill for several minutes on all sides until blackened in places. Push the meat and peppers off the skewers if you like and serve on a bed of rice on a large, warmed serving dish.

PAGODA JELLY

Preparation time: 15 minutes + several hours chilling　　　　Serves 6–8

425 g can of lychees

juice of 3 oranges

juice of 1 lemon

50 g (2 oz) caster sugar

8 teaspoons gelatine

300 ml (½ pint) creamed smatana or soured cream

240 g carton of Greek yogurt

I have still to travel in China, but excellent Chinese food can be found all over the world so that it is impossible not to be influenced by it. It was when I was first married and lived in New York that I realised how much more there was to Chinese food than the occasional glutinous chop suey I had tasted as a child. The only thing which always disappoints me is the lack of variety of sweets to end the meal. Banana and apple fritters can be delicious and lychees are one fruit which are very good canned, but I always feel that restaurant chefs should do something more imaginative with them than so obviously emptying a can into a bowl. Since the following recipe is made with milk products which the Chinese do not use, no Chinese restaurant is likely to take it up. But for those of us who can mix our cuisines it is a delicate, white, jellied mousse which has a creamy orangey yogurt base and is dotted with succulent, scented lychees.

Pagoda Jelly

Drain the juices from the lychees into a saucepan and leave the lychees on one side. Add the orange and lemon juice and the caster sugar to the saucepan. Heat the juices, sprinkle in the gelatine and stir over a gentle heat until it is dissolved. Then pour into a mixing bowl and leave until cold and just beginning to set.

Stir the mixture round and then stir in the creamed smatana or soured cream and the yogurt. Add the reserved lychees and pour into a 1.2 litre (2–pint) metal bombe or jelly mould. Chill in the fridge for several hours or overnight until very firmly set.

Dip the mould momentarily in a sink of very hot water and turn it out with a shake on to a serving plate (a dark coloured plate looks most effective with the white jelly).

Javanese Chicken with Avocado

*Chilli and Peanut Pork
Kebabs*

JAVANESE CHICKEN WITH AVOCADO

Preparation time: 30 minutes + 1 hour cooking   Serves 4

125 g (4 oz) desiccated
coconut

450 ml (¾ pint) hot water

1 lemon

3 tablespoons groundnut oil

2 teaspoons ground cumin

4 teaspoons ground coriander

5–6 cloves of garlic,
chopped

150 ml (¼ pint) water

2 level tablespoons smooth
peanut butter

1 teaspoon oyster sauce

2–3 fresh green chillies,
de-seeded and chopped

4 teaspoons brown sugar

4 chicken breast fillets,
skinned and cut in half

2 small–medium-size
onions, sliced

1 large avocado

salt

To serve:

a few whole coriander leaves
or continental parsley

Oven temperature:
Gas Mark 4/180°C/350°F

*We had taken the night train from Jakarta to Yogy-
akarta in the centre of Java. In the crush to board the
train I had all my traveller's cheques stolen and we
then had to sit up all night on wooden seats, stopping
constantly. I began to hate Java. But soon after we
arrived our luck changed when we went to visit an old
lady whose daughter I had met in Jakarta. Mrs Sahir
was tiny, with a neat black bun, humorous eyes and a
turned-up nose. She laughed a lot and took us every-
where; to the Sultan's Palace, to the temples, even to
her husband's grave which she visited every day. She
also took us to her house and gave us some of the best
food we had had so far on our trip. This chicken dish,
made with spicy peanut sauce and coconut milk, is just
a memory of the flavours we tasted, but it is a delicious
one. Serve it with rice or Chinese noodles and a salad.*

Preheat the oven. Put the coconut into a bowl
and pour in the hot water. Leave on one side.
Cut the lemon in half, squeeze out the juice and
set it aside and then, using a sharp knife, cut the
peel into thin strips. Put 2 tablespoons of the oil
into a large iron or other flameproof casserole
and heat it over a medium heat. Add the ground
cumin and coriander, stir, and then add the
chopped garlic. Stir for about a minute until the
garlic just browns. Remove from the heat. Then
add the water, the peanut butter, the oyster sauce,
the lemon juice and peel, the chopped chillies,
the brown sugar and a sprinkling of salt. Stir
until the sauce is smoothly mixed. Now add the
pieces of chicken and stir around to coat them
with sauce. Put the casserole back on the heat,
cover it, and bring the sauce just to bubbling.
Then put in the centre of the preheated oven for
1 hour.

Towards the end of the cooking, pour the
coconut and the water into a food processor and
whizz them for a minute or two; then pour them
into a sieve over a bowl. Using your hands,
squeeze out handfuls of the coconut mush as

firmly as you can over the sieve, forcing out as much 'milk' as possible until you have squeezed out all the liquid. Keep the coconut milk on one side. Heat the remaining tablespoon of oil in a frying pan over a medium heat. Add the sliced onions and fry, stirring them around frequently for several minutes until they are completely soft. Turn off the heat, leaving the onions in the pan.

When the chicken is ready, remove from the oven and stir the coconut milk into the casserole. Put it back on the heat on top of the stove, bring to the boil and let it bubble for 2–3 minutes, stirring, to thicken it slightly. Remove the casserole from the heat and cover. Cut the avocado in half, peel it and remove the stone, and cut the halves across in thin slices. Add the slices to the casserole and gently stir them in. Then add the fried onions, leaving them mostly on top. Just before serving, scatter a few coriander leaves or some continental parsley on top.

EXOTIC RAVIOLI

Preparation time: 1 hour   Serves 4–5

For the filling:

2 tablespoons groundnut oil

1 medium-size onion (a red one if possible), chopped finely

1 teaspoon ground cinnamon

1 teaspoon ground cumin

1 teaspoon paprika

½ teaspoon cayenne pepper

175 g (6 oz) skinless chicken breast, chopped very small

grated rind of a small lemon

1 level tablespoon peanut butter

salt to taste

For the dough:

250 g (8 oz) strong plain flour, plus extra for kneading

½ teaspoon salt

2 large eggs (size 1–2)

1 tablespoon milk

For the sauce:

2 teaspoons cornflour

2 tablespoons milk

250 g (8 oz) natural yogurt

1 level teaspoon black onion seeds

¼ teaspoon cayenne pepper

a small handful of roughly chopped fresh coriander or mint leaves

salt

Here is a real mixture of cultures; this heartening dish of home-made ravioli is not as Italian as it looks. The spicy chicken stuffing of the egg pasta 'pillows' owes something to North Africa, India and Indonesia. But this should not really seem incongruous since forms of pasta have been eaten in the East for centuries and it is only a European habit to assume that it must always be Italian. Ravioli can easily be made at home without a machine. The 'pillows' are bigger and more untidy in shape than the commercial types but I think they taste far better.

Heat the oil in a large frying pan. Add the chopped onion and stir it over a fairly high heat for a few minutes until softened. Turn down the heat a little and add the ground spices including the cayenne pepper. Stir, and then add the chopped chicken. Toss it around until it is sealed and add the grated lemon rind, the peanut butter and salt to taste. Stir and cook for another minute or two. Remove from the heat and leave to cool.

Meanwhile, make the pasta dough. Put the flour, salt, eggs and milk into a food processor and whizz until the mixture has stuck together into a dough. Then knead with both hands on a smooth surface, stretching the dough and pushing it back with the palms of your hands for about 10 minutes until it is smooth and elastic. Cover it in cling film and leave it to rest for about 15 minutes. Roll out the dough very thinly on a floured surface into a large rectangle. Cut it in half and spoon little piles of chicken mixture on one half of the pasta about 4 cm (1½ inches) apart. Brush between the piles with a wet pastry brush to moisten the pasta (diagram 1). Lay the second sheet of pasta on top and then, using a fluted pastry cutter or a knife, cut between the piles of filling to make your ravioli (diagram 2). Make sure the edges of the ravioli are firmly sealed, by pressing them together.

Put a large saucepan of salted water on to boil, and, meanwhile, start to prepare the sauce. Mix the cornflour in a cup with the milk and pour into a small saucepan. Add the yogurt and onion seed and season with salt and cayenne pepper. Leave on one side. When the water is boiling, drop in the ravioli, cover the pan and boil for 12 minutes. Meanwhile, bring the sauce to the boil, stirring with a wooden spoon, and then bubble it gently, still stirring, for 2–3 minutes. Cover the pan and leave it until the ravioli is ready. Then drain the ravioli and pile them in a heated serving dish. Pour over the yogurt sauce, sprinkle with the chopped coriander or mint leaves, and serve at once.

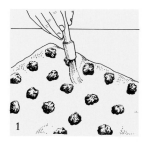 

ANGLO-CHINESE PIE

For the filling:

3 tablespoons groundnut oil

500 g (1 lb) boneless turkey breast, sliced thinly

500 g (1 lb) boneless pork shoulder steaks, sliced thinly

2 large cloves of garlic, chopped finely

5 cm (2-inch) piece of root ginger, chopped finely

¼ teaspoon cayenne pepper

300 ml (½ pint) water

1½ tablespoons soft dark brown sugar

4 tablespoons tomato ketchup

2 tablespoons tomato purée

1 tablespoon rich soy sauce

1 tablespoon wine vinegar

1 level tablespoon cornflour

230 g (8 oz) can of water chestnuts, drained and sliced thinly

salt

For the pastry:

175 g (6 oz) strong plain flour, plus extra for rolling

½ teaspoon salt

125 g (4 oz) ground rice

3 tablespoons sesame seeds

75 g (3 oz) butter

125 g (4 oz) white vegetable fat

At first sight this is a deception. What looks like a traditional, hearty English pie is put on the table. Then you look closer and see that the crisp pastry is studded with sesame seeds. Once cut, the crust reveals a golden sweet and sour mixture of turkey, pork and water chestnuts, smelling wonderful. I serve the pie with rice and a salad; it makes a popular family meal.

Preheat the oven to the first setting. Heat 2 tablespoons of the oil in a large frying pan over a high heat. Add the turkey and pork slices and stir around just to seal them all over. Then turn down the heat, and, using a slotted spatula, transfer the meat to a casserole and leave it on one side.

Add the remaining tablespoon of oil to the pan and stir the chopped garlic and ginger around over a fairly low heat for about 2 minutes. Then stir in the cayenne pepper, the water, the brown sugar, the tomato ketchup and purée, the soy sauce and the vinegar. Remove the pan from the heat. Mix the cornflour in a cup with 2 tablespoons of water and stir it until smooth. Add this to the pan mixture, put the pan back on the heat and stir it constantly until it is bubbling and thickened. Continue stirring for about 2 minutes. Then pour the sauce into the casserole with the meat, stir it in and cover the casserole. Put the dish in the centre of the oven for 20 minutes and then turn down the heat to the second setting and cook for another hour.

Remove the casserole from the oven and add a little salt to taste. Stir the water chestnut slices into the meat mixture. Then turn the filling into a 1.2–1.5-litre (2–2½-pint) traditional pie dish and leave until cold.

Meanwhile, prepare the pastry. Sift the flour, salt and ground rice into a bowl. Stir in the sesame seeds. Add the butter and fat, cut into small pieces, and rub them in lightly (or do it all

a little groundnut oil

Oven temperatures:
Gas Mark 8/230°C/450°F
Gas Mark 1/150°C/275°F
Gas Mark 6/200°C/400°F

in a food processor). Stir in 3–4 tablespoons of very cold water with a knife until the mixture only just begins to stick together. Then press the dough into a ball and roll it out on a floured surface into a piece big enough to cover the pie dish. Moisten the edges of the pie dish and lay the pastry on it. Cut round the edge neatly and mark it all around with the back of a knife. Roll out the pastry trimmings and cut them into shapes to decorate the top of the pie. Make two small incisions to allow steam to escape. Refrigerate the pie for 30 minutes or more and preheat the oven to the third setting. Just before cooking, brush the pie crust lightly with cold water and a little groundnut oil. Cook it in the centre of the oven for 25–30 minutes until browned.

INDIA AND BURMA

QUAILS IN RICH, RED, INDIAN SAUCE

Preparation time: 30 minutes + 2 hours cooking · Serves 6

2–3 fresh green chillies, de-seeded and chopped roughly

1 large red pepper, de-seeded and chopped roughly

2 large cloves of garlic

2 medium–large onions, chopped roughly

75 g (3 oz) butter

1 teaspoon ground cinnamon

½ teaspoon ground cloves

1 teaspoon ground coriander

1 teaspoon ground fennel seed

½ tablespoon tamarind concentrate or 1 tablespoon lemon juice

300 ml (½ pint) boiling water, if using tamarind concentrate

397 g (14 oz) can of chopped tomatoes

1 tablespoon tomato purée

50 g (2 oz) sultanas

2 teaspoons black onion seeds (optional)

6 quails

4–5 tablespoons natural yogurt

salt

Oven temperature:
Gas Mark 3/170°C/325°F

Quails are often eaten in India, and, since tasting them there, I find it difficult to resist cooking all game birds in an Indian style because it works so well. In this dish, I cook the little birds slowly in a thick and wonderful sauce so that the sauce is as much a part of the dish as the quails. Served with plenty of rice, either basmati or brown, you should only need one bird each as the long cooking ensures that you get every piece of flesh off the bones and there is plenty of sauce. As a green vegetable, a mixture of sliced leeks and petits pois goes well with this. If possible, buy the spices whole and grind them in a coffee grinder or with a pestle and mortar. This rather special dish is extremely simple to make.

Preheat the oven. Put the prepared chillies, red pepper, garlic and onions into a food processor and whizz until they are chopped to a very smooth purée. Melt the butter in an iron or other flameproof casserole over a medium heat. Add the ground spices and stir them around. Then add the vegetable purée and leave it bubbling over a low heat, stirring occasionally, for 8–10 minutes.

Meanwhile, dissolve the tamarind concentrate in a measuring jug with the boiling water. Add the tamarind water, the canned tomatoes and the tomato purée to the casserole. Season it with salt. Bring this thick sauce to the boil and add the sultanas, and the onion seeds if you are using them. Then add the quails. Cover the dish, and cook it in the centre of the oven for 1¼–2 hours. Lastly, spoon the yogurt on top of the curry, but don't stir it in, and put the lid of the casserole on again for a few minutes to warm the yogurt.

Quails in Rich, Red, Indian Sauce

PRIDE OF THE PUNJAB

Preparation time: 45 minutes + 2 hours marinating   Serves 6–7
+ 1¼ hours cooking

2 pinches of saffron strands
or 1 packet of powdered
saffron

1 tablespoon hot water

6 rounded tablespoons
natural yogurt

2 large cloves of garlic,
chopped finely

2.5 cm–5 cm (1–2-inch)
piece of root ginger, chopped
finely

50 g (2 oz) butter

1.75 kg (4 lb) chicken,
skinned

1 teaspoon ground cumin

1 teaspoon ground cinnamon

½ teaspoon ground
cardamom

½ teaspoon ground cloves

½ teaspoon ground mace

¼–½ teaspoon cayenne
pepper

¼ of a whole nutmeg,
grated

1 tablespoon groundnut or
sunflower oil

2 large onions, peeled,
halved and sliced finely

300 ml (½ pint) chicken
stock

a few coriander leaves or
continental parsley

Oven temperature:
Gas Mark 3/170°C/325°F

*In India, chicken is expensive and a whole bird is
usually only served for a rather special occasion. The
cooking of north India is less fiery than that of the
south; dishes tend to be aromatically spiced rather than
hot. Chicken is often marinated in yogurt and spices
and the results are wonderful. For us, a chicken is one
of the less expensive Sunday offerings and can be a bit
dull. This way of cooking it will transform an ordinary
battery bird into a dish fit for a banquet.*

Soak the saffron in the hot water for at least 5
minutes. Put 4 tablespoons of the yogurt into a
bowl and mix in the chopped garlic and ginger
and the saffron with its water. Then stir in all the
spices. Put the chicken in a shallow pan or dish.
Spoon a tablespoon of the yogurt mixture into
the body cavity of the chicken and smear the rest
all over the bird. Leave at room temperature for
1–2 hours.

Preheat the oven. In a large iron or other
flameproof casserole on top of the stove heat the
butter and oil over a medium heat. Add the
sliced onions and sauté until they are soft. Then
remove them with a slotted spoon and put them
on one side. Now put the chicken in the
casserole and lightly brown it to seal on all sides.
Return the onions to the dish and scrape in any
remaining marinade from the chicken. Add the
chicken stock, bring to the boil, cover and cook
in the centre of the oven for 30 minutes. Then
turn the chicken over so that it is breast-side
down. Cover again and continue to cook for
another 45 minutes.

Take out the chicken, put it into a serving dish
right-side-up, and put it in a low oven to keep
warm. On top of the stove, boil the juices and
onion in the casserole rapidly for about 10
minutes until reduced by half, stirring now and
then. Remove from the heat and stir in the

remaining 2 rounded tablespoons of yogurt.
Season if necessary. Just before serving, pour the
thick sauce all over the chicken and sprinkle a
few coriander leaves on top.

CHICKEN NOODLES WITH CASHEW NUTS IN THE BURMESE WAY

Preparation time: 40 minutes + 10 minutes cooking   Serves 4–5

2 large skinless chicken
breasts

2 tablespoons oyster sauce

1 level tablespoon soft dark
brown sugar

3–4 pinches of cayenne
pepper

250 g (8 oz) Chinese egg
noodles

350 g (12 oz) carrots

2 tablespoons groundnut oil

2.5 cm (1-inch) piece of root
ginger, peeled and chopped
finely

2 cloves of garlic, chopped
finely

1 teaspoon ground turmeric

75 g (3 oz) unsalted cashew
nuts

leaves of a small–medium-
size bunch of fresh
coriander, chopped finely

*The seven precious days which a tourist's visa allows
you in Burma are an intense and unique experience. It
is so fascinating that you seem to find extra energy to
help pack the time with sights and events, and so make
the most of every second. There is no time to sit lazily
over a meal but snack food in Burma, as in many
Eastern countries, is excellent and in the markets we
always found little establishments where you could eat
a bowl of noodles with chicken and vegetables. This is
a quick all-in-one family meal, for a hurried lunch or
supper.*

Cut the chicken breasts across in thin slices and
put them in a bowl with 1 tablespoon of the
oyster sauce, the brown sugar and the cayenne
pepper. Stir the slices to coat them evenly, cover
the bowl and leave to marinate while you
prepare the other ingredients. Cook the noodles
according to the directions on the packet, drain
them and leave them on one side. Peel and slice
the carrots very finely, using a food processor if
possible. Put the oil in a wok or a large iron or
other flameproof casserole over a medium heat.
Add the chopped ginger and garlic, the turmeric
and the cashew nuts and stir around for a
minute. Then add the marinated chicken and stir
around for 3–4 minutes, until the chicken is just
cooked. Add the sliced carrots, stir for another
minute, and, lastly, add the reserved noodles
and the remaining tablespoon of oyster sauce;
stir until everything is just warmed through.
Very roughly mix in the coriander leaves and
serve immediately.

A PUDDING FOR PARVATI

2 tablespoons caster sugar

75 g (3 oz) flaked almonds

1 teaspoon ground
cardamom

125 g (4 oz) semolina

6 tablespoons powdered milk

900 ml (1½ pints) milk

175 g (6 oz) demerara sugar

125 g (4 oz) carrots, grated

juice of 1 lemon, strained

1 tablespoon rose-water

Would this be fit for the Hindu goddess Parvati? I hope so. It has characteristics drawn from the many different types of Indian sweetmeats, being milky, scented and intriguingly textured, but not so intensely sweet. I am afraid that I have a very sweet tooth and I always return fatter, rather than thinner, after a visit to India. I do think that a little sharpness combines with sweetness to make an even better taste, though, which is why I often add lemon juice to Eastern-style puddings.

Sprinkle the caster sugar evenly over the bottom of a 1.2 litre (2-pint) capacity shallow mould or flan dish. Then sprinkle 50 g (2 oz) of the flaked almonds over the sugar. Heat a heavy-based saucepan over a medium heat, add the ground cardamom and stir for a moment or two to roast it. Remove the pan from the heat and after a minute or two add the semolina and powdered milk. Pour in 150 ml (¼ pint) milk and stir to mix smoothly. Then add the demerara sugar and gradually stir in the remaining 750 ml (1¼ pints) of milk. Now add the grated carrots. Put the pan back over a medium heat and bring to the boil, stirring all the time. Lower the heat and bubble, stirring constantly, for 10–12 minutes, until very thick. Then remove from the heat and gradually stir in the lemon juice and rose-water. Mix in the remaining 25 g (1 oz) flaked almonds and pour the mixture into the prepared mould or flan dish. Leave to cool and then chill thoroughly in the fridge for several hours.

To turn out, loosen the edges with your fingers and then turn on to a serving plate, giving a good shake. Now put the cake under a medium grill until it is darkly speckled on top. Chill again in the fridge before serving it cut into pieces.

A Pudding for Parvati
Sweet Rice Balls in Scented Cream

SWEET RICE BALLS IN SCENTED CREAM

Preparation time: 35 minutes + 30 minutes chilling   Serves 6–10

For the rice balls:

600 ml (1 pint) milk

75 g (3 oz) milk powder

a few strands of saffron (optional)

75 g (3 oz) pudding rice

50 g (2 oz) soft light brown sugar

½ level teaspoon ground cardamom

15 g (½ oz) butter

25 g (1 oz) unsalted cashew nuts

25 g (1 oz) sultanas

about 25 g (1 oz) desiccated coconut

For the cream:

300 ml (½ pint) milk

50 g (2 oz) milk powder

2 teaspoons caster sugar

1 tablespoon rose-water

Some of the Indian sweets are too sweet even for my shamefully sweet tooth but a few of the concentrated milk sweetmeats, flavoured with cardamom and rose-water, are completely irresistible. Bengalis are the great sweetmeat makers and in Calcutta you see shops and stalls laden with an extraordinary variety. It's quite fun occasionally to make some at home. I treat them more like chocolates to eat after the meal than as a pudding, and they are a good accompaniment to fresh fruit. These are simply my invention, but they have an absolutely authentic taste which for me always evokes nostalgia for India.

To make the rice balls, put the milk into a heavy saucepan and sprinkle in the milk powder. Stir to mix and add the saffron, if used. Add the rice and bring the milk to the boil, stirring all the time. Then simmer gently, stirring almost constantly, for about 15 minutes until very thick. Now stir in the brown sugar and the ground cardamom and remove the pan from the heat. Melt the butter in a frying pan over a medium heat. Add the cashew nuts and stir around for a moment or two just until the nuts are beginning to brown, add the sultanas and stir for a moment or two more until they are puffing up and browning. Stir the nuts and sultanas into the rice mixture and then turn everything into a bowl, cover it and leave until the mixture is completely cold, about 30 minutes.

Meanwhile, make the cream. Put the milk in a saucepan and add the milk powder and the caster sugar. Stir over a low heat, just to dissolve the milk powder and sugar and immediately remove from the heat. Stir in the rose-water and leave until cold. When the rice mixture is cold, roll it into walnut-sized balls in your hands and then roll these lightly in desiccated coconut. Arrange the balls in a fairly shallow serving dish – metal or glass looks best – and pour the scented cream all over them.

BURMESE FISH CURRY

Preparation time: 30 minutes + 15 minutes cooking   Serves 6

5 tablespoons groundnut oil, plus a little extra

1 teaspoon turmeric

2 teaspoons salt

1–1.15 kg (2¼–2½ lb) cod fillet

5 cm (2-inch) piece of root ginger, chopped finely

2 large cloves of garlic, chopped finely

250 g (8 oz) tomatoes, skinned and chopped small

½ teaspoon cayenne pepper

1 good tablespoon oyster sauce

450 ml (¾ pint) water

juice of 1 lemon

a bunch of spring onions, cut in 5 cm (2-inch) pieces

Arriving in Rangoon seemed like going back in time. I could see no modern buildings, and of the few cars the latest model looked circa 1950. As we travelled around Burma for the tantalising seven days which our visa allowed us, we felt a peace and gentleness which has long since disappeared from modern life as we know it. We had dinner one evening with a family in their teak house on stilts near Mandalay. Burmese food is like a mixture of Chinese and Indian, which to me is a good combination. I also loved eating so much fish. The Burmese would add more chillies or cayenne pepper to the following curry, so if you have fiery tastes you can do so too. Serve with plenty of rice, boiled potatoes or Chinese noodles to soak up the delicious juices. I find steamed whole-leaf spinach is a particularly good vegetable for this dish.

In a large mixing bowl, put 3 tablespoons groundnut oil, the turmeric and the salt and stir them together. Skin the cod and cut it into large chunks. Put the fish into the mixing bowl and rub it all over with the oil and turmeric mixture. Heat a thin film of oil in a large frying pan to a high heat. Then add the pieces of fish and fry for a minute on each side to seal them, turning gently. Remove from the heat and set aside.

Pour any remaining oil and turmeric from the mixing bowl into an iron or other flameproof casserole and add the remaining 2 tablespoons groundnut oil. Heat to a medium heat. Add the chopped ginger and garlic and stir them around for a minute or two until just beginning to brown. Add the chopped tomatoes and the cayenne pepper and stir over the heat for another 2 minutes. Stir in the oyster sauce and then remove the pan from the heat. Add the water and lemon juice and stir before carefully adding the fish and any pan juices. Cover the casserole and allow it just to bubble over a very low heat for 15 minutes. Add the spring onions, cover, and cook for another 2–3 minutes.

PERFECT POTATOES – INDIAN STYLE

Preparation and cooking time: 25 minutes   Serves 4–5

750 g (1½ lb) medium–large potatoes

2 large cloves of garlic

2.5 cm (1-inch) piece of root ginger

2 tablespoons groundnut oil

25 g (1 oz) butter

2 teaspoons ground cinnamon

3 teaspoons ground coriander

4 teaspoons whole caraway seeds

½ teaspoon cayenne pepper

4 tablespoons chopped parsley

sea salt

To me this is an irresistible way of eating potatoes. Although they are spicy and aromatic there is no need to keep them solely for an exotic meal: they will also greatly enhance your Sunday roast. If you have any left over they are good eaten cold, but don't put them in the fridge because this spoils the cooked potatoes. During the summer they can be an interesting picnic ingredient, eaten in your fingers. If you have one, a wok is ideal for sautéing the potatoes in.

Scrub the potatoes but don't peel them. Cut them into roughly 2.5 cm (1-inch) cubes. Steam or boil them until they are just cooked but not falling to bits. Then peel the garlic and ginger and chop them finely together. Heat the oil and butter in a large frying pan or a wok over a medium heat. Add the chopped garlic and ginger, stir around for about 2 minutes, and then add all the spices, including the cayenne pepper and stir for another minute. Add the potatoes and sauté over a medium heat for about 8 minutes. Then stir in a sprinkling of sea salt and the chopped parsley, remove from the heat and turn into a heated serving dish.

Burmese Fish Curry

Perfect Potatoes –
Indian Style

egetarian Indian

89

THE VEGETARIAN INDIAN

1 teaspoon cumin seeds

2 teaspoons coriander seeds

1 heaped teaspoon tamarind concentrate, or 4 teaspoons lemon juice

2 tablespoons groundnut oil

25 g (1 oz) butter

2–3 cloves of garlic, chopped

500 g (1 lb) tomatoes, chopped roughly

500 g (1 lb) fresh spinach, washed thoroughly

2 teaspoons mustard seeds (optional)

1/4 teaspoon cayenne pepper

432 g (15 1/4 oz) can of chick-peas, drained

4 medium–large eggs (size 2–3)

1 rounded tablespoon desiccated coconut

salt

If you are travelling in India on a limited budget – which in that country I feel is much the most interesting thing to do – you nearly always eat best if you stick to the vegetarian dishes. Chicken is delicious in India but it is expensive, and meat is often very tough indeed. The variety of vegetable dishes can make a very satisfying meal. This recipe for spinach and chick-peas cooked in spices and tamarind with eggs is substantial enough to be a complete supper dish.

Put the cumin and coriander seeds in a coffee grinder and grind them finely. Mix the tamarind concentrate with 2 tablespoons of very hot water in a cup stirring with a teaspoon until smooth. Put the oil and butter in an iron or other flameproof casserole dish and heat them over a medium heat. Add the garlic and ground spices and stir for a minute; add the chopped tomatoes and bubble, stirring all the time, for about 5 minutes until the tomatoes have softened to a mush.

Stir in the tamarind juice or lemon juice and then put in the whole leaves of spinach (you needn't both to take off the stalks). Cover the casserole and cook over a medium heat for a few minutes until the spinach has gone limp. Then uncover, stir around, add the mustard seeds, the cayenne pepper, the drained chick-peas and a sprinkling of salt. Cook in the open dish over a medium to high heat for about 8 minutes, stirring around all the time.

Lower the heat, break the eggs on top of the spinach mixture, cover the dish again and cook for 6–8 minutes until the eggs are just set. Meanwhile, heat a small dry frying pan and toast the desiccated coconut for a minute or two until golden. When the eggs are ready, scatter the toasted coconut on top and serve.

SOUTH AMERICA

BRAISED BEEF IN WALNUT, CHILLI AND CHOCOLATE SAUCE

Preparation time: 40 minutes + 3 hours cooking	Serves 4–5

75 g (3 oz) walnut pieces, ground finely

1 medium–large onion, chopped roughly

3–4 green chillies, de-seeded and chopped roughly

1 large clove of garlic, chopped roughly

25 g (1 oz) raisins

4–5 cloves

1 rounded tablespoon cocoa powder

397 g (14 oz) can of tomatoes

3 tablespoons sunflower oil

1 teaspoon ground cinnamon

600 ml (1 pint) beef stock

750 g (1½ lb) lean braising beef, cubed

a bunch of spring onions, chopped, using as much of the green part as possible

salt

Oven temperature:
Gas Mark 2/150°C/300°F

Chocolate is used in savoury dishes in South America, Spain and even in Italy. It must have originated from a chocolate drink found in Mexico in the 16th century, which was unsweetened. When I went to join my parents in Peru I was amazed at the idea of chocolate being cooked with meat and thought it must be quite horrible, but in fact it just enriches the flavour. In South America there is a famous turkey dish for special occasions which has both chocolate, chillies and many other ingredients in the thick sauce. This gave me the idea for a simpler dish made along the same lines which can be eaten on any day and is particularly cheering during the winter. Since most chocolate we can buy is over-sweet I find the sauce works best made with unsweetened cocoa powder.

Preheat the oven. Put the first eight ingredients in a food processor. Whizz thoroughly until as smooth as possible. Now heat 2 tablespoons sunflower oil in a large iron or other flameproof casserole over a medium heat. Add the cinnamon and stir, and then add the mixture from the food processor and let it bubble, stirring constantly, for 5 minutes. Now stir in the stock, remove the pan from the heat and add salt to taste. Heat the remaining tablespoon of sunflower oil in a large frying pan to a very high heat. Add the beef and fry it until sealed and browned all over. Add to the sauce in the casserole, together with any pan juices. Put the casserole back on the heat and bring it to bubbling; then cover the dish and cook in the preheated oven for 2½–3 hours until the meat is tender and the sauce has reduced and thickened. Before serving, stir in the chopped spring onions.

PERUVIAN POTATOES

Preparation time: 1 hour
Serves 4–5

1 smallish onion, a red one if possible

4 tablespoons lemon juice

2 pinches of cayenne pepper

2 fresh green chillies

750 g (1½ lb) small to medium-size potatoes

2 tablespoons olive oil

175 g (6 oz) cottage cheese

150 ml (5 fl oz) carton of double cream

1 level teaspoon turmeric

4 hard-boiled eggs

salt

The best potatoes I have ever tasted came from the mountains of Peru; they had a close waxy texture and were quite a deep yellow colour. It may be only the soil or the climate of the 'Sierra' which gives them this characteristic colour, because a reader wrote to me saying that when she bought some yellow seed potatoes back from Peru to plant in England they grew well, but turned white. I remember that we used to eat these potatoes cooked 'a la Huancaina', with hard-boiled eggs and onions in a white cheese and chilli sauce with turmeric. I have attempted to reproduce it in the following recipe. The nearest thing to those Peruvian potatoes that I have been able to find are Italian waxy potatoes which have a pale yellow colour and appear in the shops here during the winter; in the summer Jersey potatoes would do well. You could serve this as an accompaniment to meat or chicken or as a light lunch dish together with a salad.

Peel the onion and slice it very thinly in rings. Put it in a shallow bowl and stir in the lemon

Peruvian Potatoes

juice, the cayenne pepper and a little salt. Cover
the bowl and leave it on one side. Cut the chillies
open under running water, discard the seeds and
stem and then chop them up very finely. Wash
but don't peel the potatoes and steam or boil
them until they are cooked but not falling apart.

Meanwhile, gently heat the olive oil in a small
pan and fry the chillies for 2–3 minutes. Put the
cottage cheese, cream and turmeric and a little
salt into a food processor, add the chillies and
pan juices and whizz until smooth. Cut the
cooked potatoes in half and arrange on a serving
dish. Peel the hard–boiled eggs, cut them in half
lengthways and arrange them amongst the
potatoes. Pour the sauce over the top, and then
drain the marinated onion rings and arrange
them on the dish.

*Passion-fruit and
Honey Soufflé*

Braised Beef in Walnut, Chilli and Chocolate Sauce

PASSION-FRUIT AND HONEY SOUFFLÉ

Preparation time: 30 minutes + 2 hours chilling   Serves 6–7

3 rounded tablespoons clear
or set honey

juice of 2 large lemons

11 g (½ oz) sachet or
3 teaspoons gelatine

4 large eggs (size 1–2)

6 passion-fruit

a pinch of salt

*Sadly, although I spent six months in Peru when I
was thirteen, I remember very little about the local
food, but one thing which remains a favourite since
that time is the sublime flavour of passion-fruit.
Another Peruvian memory is of a cook we had who
made a lot of cold and hot soufflés so I feel that this
heavenly pudding owes its inspiration to that period of
my life.*

Put the honey in a small saucepan with the
lemon juice and heat it gently. When the honey
has melted, sprinkle in the gelatine and stir over
the lowest heat (you mustn't let the mixture
boil) until the gelatine has dissolved. Remove
the pan from the heat and put it on one side.
Separate the eggs, putting the whites in a large
bowl and the yolks in the top of a double
saucepan or a bowl. Using a wooden spoon,
whisk the honey and lemon mixture briskly into
the egg yolks and put over the saucepan base or a
pan of barely simmering water. Continue stirring
all the time for 5 minutes until the mixture has
thickened slightly; then remove the pan from the
heat and put a small sieve over it. Cut open five
of the six passion-fruit and scoop the flesh into
the sieve with a teaspoon. Rub the flesh through
the sieve with a small spoon until you have got as
much juice and flesh as possible out of the seeds.
Stir into the honey and egg mixture. Then spoon
in the remaining passion-fruit, with its seeds,
and stir thoroughly. Pour into a mixing bowl
and allow to cool slightly.

Now add the salt to the egg whites and whisk
until they hold soft peaks. Gently but thoroughly
fold them into the egg yolk mixture with a metal
spoon. Pour the mixture into a pretty glass
serving bowl or individual dishes. Scatter some
of the sieved-out passion-fruit seeds on top and
refrigerate until set, about 2 hours.

Note: it is easier to measure the honey
accurately if you warm the measuring spoon.

INDEX TO RECIPES

Design and layout: Ken Vail Graphic Design
Photography: Laurie Evans
Food preparation for photography: Liz and Pete
Stylist: Lesley Richardson
Illustrations: Mandy Doyle
Typesetting: Westholme Graphics
Printed and bound by Balding & Mansell Ltd,
Wisbech, Cambs